*To those whom I was privileged
to meet along the way*

I wish to acknowledge the help and support I received in the preparation and publication of this book, particularly the following:

Dublin Corporation Personnel Department,
also Frank Kelly, Brendan Hayden.

I. M. P. A. C. T. Trade Union Committee,
also Seán Redmond, Eamonn Donnelly, John Smithers.

Dubco Credit Union Committee,
also Tom Corrigan, Monica Murphy, Margaret Muldoon, Michael Comiskey.

North East Access Radio Committee,
also Ciaran Murray, Tony Fitzsimons.

Kilmainham Gaol Museum.

Billy French, Michael Proctor, Cathleen O'Neill, Andy Kinsella, Joan O'Mara.

The Last Corporation Man

Published in 1998 by
Bobdog Publications. Tel: 01 842 0229

A CIP record is available from the British Library.

ISBN 0-9532882-0-X

Typeset by Carole Lynch
Printed by ColourBooks Ltd.,
Baldoyle Industrial Estate,
Dublin 13,
Ireland.

Contents

Introduction

After being "let go" when the job finished, I headed for the Labour in Gardiner Street, a grey building overshadowed by the tail-end of the Loopline Bridge in a run-down part of the City. Things were bad in the building game; the often-promised post war boom has so far failed to materialise, with many building workers forced to take the "boat".

The usual gathering of people congregated outside, smoking "Woodbines", the cheapest cigarettes available. Inside, the walls reflected the standard Civil Service colours, golden brown and bottle green. A series of numbered hatches, fronted with a wire grill, filled one end of the room. Queues of poorly dressed men waited stoically to be interviewed by the poe faced staff. Choosing the shortest queue, not that it made much difference, I took my place and waited my cards at the ready.

"Next please", came the dull voice of the man behind the wire.

The necessary cards were handed over to be scrutinised and examined. A file was produced and the checking began. After what appeared to be an eternity the clerk enquired.

"So you are a carpenter?"

"Yes", I replied, with no great enthusiasm, having been through this ritual before.

"Well, you are in luck today", answered yer man, "the Corpo are looking for carpenters, interested?"

"Certainly I am", was my response. One had reservations about working in the Corporation, it was not considered much of a job in the trade. Why not give it a try. The alternative was the "boat".

"Have you a Union card", asked the clerk.

"Of course I have", came my reply.

"Well, present this card along with your Union card, 8.30 a.m. tomorrow morning at the Corporation Depot in Keogh Street.

So began for me, a 40-year odyssey into a strange, bizarre, amusing and sometimes tragic world. It was, on reflection, almost a kind of sub-culture life I never knew existed in my own native city. To work with, to sup with, to observe some very

1

ordinary people and some of the most extraordinary characters one could hope to find anywhere. This is a personal account, for me a voyage of discovery. I have endeavoured to recall the people, the situations and the conditions of that time. Each of the characters, in their own way, contributed to a truly amazing time of life under the most trying and difficulty conditions, yet somehow managed to survive. In the end that's what it was all about, survival.

A Paint Job in East Wall 1957/8
Joe Claffey, John Southworth (the Englishman) and Vincent Flood.

A Paint Job

Always, when starting a new job, one approaches it with a certain degree of excitement and apprehension. And, so it was that faithful morning when he was instructed to report to the Joiner's Shop in Shamrock Terrace, North Strand. Collecting his toolbox and, securing it to the bike, he headed off.

It turned out to be a small workshop with four or five benches and some woodworking machines. There was seven joiners working in pairs, the odd man out was to be his new mate. It was normal to work with a complete stranger for a day or so, depending on the type of work being carried out.

3

The Foreman introduced him to John Southworth. His very name implied he was different, he certainly was. An anomaly, an Englishman working in Dublin in the '50s. A grey-haired man of medium build from Yorkshire, his accent caused some problems. He had a strange way of looking at you, with one eye closed, like someone wearing a monocle. Needless to say he was nicknamed "Tight-Eye", but never to his face.

His wry sense of humour did not always appeal to some of the other craftsmen. He was the first foreigner Dave had ever met, his perception of the English was distorted by the history taught in school, he had been conditioned to dislike, even hate, anything English. A more unlikely pair you could not find, a middle-aged Yorkshire atheist and him an impressionable young man, but somehow it worked, they got on great together.

The work was mundane, repetitive assembly-line joinery, mostly doors and windows, with an occasional stairs to break the routine. It afforded them plenty of time to talk, should I say John to talk, Dave to Listen. John would speak at great length an authority on many subjects, of things Dave knew precious little, literature, music, world affairs, most of all about people. For an unbeliever, John was the most Christian man Dave had ever met.

He introduced Dave to a world of Orwell, A.J. Cronin, Steinbeck, Raymond Chandler, to mention but a few. He explained in great detail the significance of literature. He left Dave with an abiding love of books and writing. He lent Dave books to study and read; some he could understand, others were over his head. One book in particular opened his eyes to the appalling system of Apartheid in South Africa, long before it became fashionable. Another book he spoke highly of was 'The Ragged Trousered Philanthropist' by an Irishman, Robert Tresell, a copy of which Dave managed to acquire some years later in London.

John would speak at relish on the decline of the British Empire since the last war and various other parts of the same Empire where the influence had been so evident. For an Englishman he was very critical of his country's part in world affairs.

Dave knew nothing of the history or culture of any other country, whether that was his fault or the system of education he still does not know. There were so many areas covered in the course of their discussions, it was incredible. So was Dave's total lack of understanding; John never once remarked on Dave's ignorance or lack of knowledge; for Dave it was an eye-opener.

Dave began to realise how closed and claustrophobic his upbringing had been; you just accepted things as they were, never questioning. It came as a shock to realise that there were other things in the world besides football. Religion was rarely mentioned. Only once did John inquire as to how someone like Dave received bread and wine at Communion and him a confirmed tea-totaller. Dave's explanation was received without comment, just a nod of the head.

John's presence in Ireland he explained, was due to a refusal on his part to join the Army, having lost his father in the Great War, it was in keeping with the character of the man, as to his marital status, he never said – Dave never asked.

John's all consuming passion was horseracing – his spare time and spare cash was devoted to the "Gee-Gees".

Studying form, always searching for that elusive big winner, doubles, trebles, cross-doubles, 'Yankees' three-penny up and down trebles, every conceivable type of bet. He held long and detailed discussions with like minded work mates on the merits and demerits of this horse or that jockey. If he ever managed to make any money Dave never knew, John kept his council to himself. Dave can still see him on a cold morning in the unheated workshop; his trousers tucked into his socks, a woollen scarf wrapped tightly round his neck. His bony hands in mittens, topped off with a black beret pulled down round his ears, as he tried to keep the heat in and the cold out.

It is a little unfair to make comparisons with the other Tradesmen, their skills were equal, but intellectually John was in a different league. They were mates for about 18 months, a long time indeed, not for Dave, he enjoyed every moment of it. It was like a light had been switched on in his head.

With a down-turn in Joinery work, they were both transferred to a 'Paint Job', (repairs before painting), in East wall. So, collecting their tools, they headed off on their bikes. Up Newcomen Bridge, down the Ossary Road and on to St Mary's Road in search of the Hut!

Opposite the school they entered a narrow passageway leading to an open yard behind the houses. A food centre for the poor occupied one section, beside which was erected one of the infamous 'Nissan' Hut. To say that it had seen better days was an understatement, there were so many holes in the roof that when it rained it was considered to be drier outside.

Parking their bikes against the hut they rambled inside to report to the Foreman. A large rectangular trestle table sat in the centre of the floor with bench seats running parallel. At the dark end of the hut a home-made desk standing like a church refectory, complete with raised dais, to give the Foreman a head and shoulders advantage when he addressed the assembled crew each morning. New doors and sashes were stacked neatly and carefully utilising the remaining space.

Two men who were standing talking turned at their entrance. "We are to report to Christy McCoy", stated John in his broad Yorkshire accent that raised a few eyebrows.

"He's not here at the moment", answered one of the men; "He'll be back in a few minutes: where did youse come from".

"The Strand, been in the workshop, for a few months" replied Dave. "What's it like here".

"Handy enough once you get used to it", said one of the men, a stocky man with a well lined face and straight black shining hair that smelt of 'Brylcreem'. "Take a seat".

Before they could attempt a sit down a bent old man appeared in the door ope. He had the most wrinkled, weather-beaten face ever seen, the bags under his bloodshot eyes were like a pair of wet socks hanging on a clothesline. John immediately stepped forward, hand outstretched.

"Christy McCoy, I presume", he asked firmly.

The old man, on hearing the strange accent, raised his bloodshot eyes to heaven.

"Sorry, mate, wrong spy", he answered in a fair imitation on the Yorkshire accent. "I'm only the Labourer round here".

Archie Cruickshank was an old soldier who had served in the British Army for many years, spending most of his service in India, hence the wrinkled face. It had done nothing for his temperament, a grumpy, foul-mouthed and unhappy man who, when provoked, which was often, would light up the sky with the most colourful language, in his case it was true what they say about old soldiers.

His principle duties were to deliver the materials required to houses due for repair by means of an old handcart, almost as ancient as himself. Of more immediate concern to the crew was the boiling of water in the preparation of tea. Naturally his services were in demand when it came to laying bets at the local 'Bookies' shop.

"If you want tea, you better hand in your 'Billy Cans'", he snapped "or you won't get any tea this morning".

Dutifully they handed over their respective cans, each with their own distinctive marking, a twisted nail, a piece of copper wire, some were even name-stamped. At that moment the Foreman arrived.

"I take it you are the real McCoy" asked John with a glint in his eye.

"You can say that again", answered Christy, "two real Joiners, the right men in the right place".

"What's the score", enquired Dave, trying to assess the situation. "I have a number of doors to be repaired", said Christy. "Some of them here couldn't join their hands, never mind doors; after the tea-break I'll show you what's to be done".

He was a round faced man with the standard flat cap, who in his spare time played trombone in a marching band, acting in a temporary capacity as a Foreman. His position was an impossible post to fill. Never knowing from one job to another if he would be 'standing up' or back on his tools the result of which, if he tried to impost a strict regime, he could find himself back on his tools with the same crew at some future date.

Shortly afterwards Christy went outside and gave a blast from his whistle to summons the troops for the tea break. Before he could remove the whistle from his lips they came in a rush of bodies, in all shapes and sizes; it was obvious they had been waiting for the signal. A large crew it was too, almost 30 carpenters in number. Dave had never seen so many old men on one job before. All were wearing some form of headgear, caps, hats; one old timer sported a bowler hat and a white apron. Most were past their prime but somehow managed to retain a certain air of dignity of an age past when being a tradesman inferred a place in society.

The cans were soon sorted out, not for them the communal bucket they being individuals, certainly respecting the Labourer but at the same time keeping him at a distance. They drank their tea, ate their sandwiches, smoked their pipes and spoke of old times and the many builders, both good and bad, they had worked for. The few young men naturally dined together, their needs were more immediate; all the heavy work like hanging new doors was carried out by them, only as it should be.

When an area was due for painting, (officially called 'Repairs before Painting', nicknamed 'A Paint Job'), mostly every 5-7 years a survey of each house was carried out, a list was compiled of the necessary work to be carried out. Only the outside of the houses was painted; doors, windows, gutters and railings, replacement windows and doors were ordered and, in due course, delivered on site. The carpenters carried out the work as stated on each docket, any extra work had to be sanctioned by the Foreman. If, in the course of work, an extra door was required the Foreman, rather than order a new door which could take months to prepare, would decide to repair the defective door on site.

That's where John and Dave came in. Their experience in the Joiner Shop made them ideal candidates. Also, they had the tools for this work, most of the carpenters on a 'Paint Job' only required a limited number of tools.

Christy handed John a docket detailing repairs to a hall door; a new bottom rail was needed. First Dave went with the redoubtable Archie to take down the door and replace it with a temporary door. The door was loaded on to the handcart and returned to the Hut.

A workbench was set up to facilitate the necessary repairs. The fact that John was an Englishman was never an issue, most of the men had at some time or other worked in England. He was treated with the utmost courtesy and respect, they had all one thing in common – horses – John was no more successful than the others were.

With the materials delivered and the hut swept out Archie set about one of his less desirable chores. The dry toilet housed in a small extension to the rear of the hut had to be emptied out. This necessitated the lifting of a manhole cover close to the hut and the filthy contents of the toilet unceremoniously dumped into it, for which the grand sum of 2/(10) a day 'dirty money' was awarded.

Around a quarter to one o'clock the men began to appear on the street in anticipation of the whistle. When it did sound off the 'Boys of the Old Brigade' arrived post haste, the front runners claimed the available seats, latecomers had to make do as best as they could, weather permitting, most preferred to eat outside. An ongoing card game of 'Spoil 15' resumed its course, with a pool that had accumulated over a number of days making it a very desirable prize. As each card was played great attention was afforded the next player, wondering was he playing for himself or for the table; woe betide the one who ventured a short corner into the dealer in the hope of scooping the pool. On each occasion the dealer had managed to hammer the card, thus prolonging the game; sooner or later the prize would be won but for the moment it was safe.

Christy banging on the table brought the noisy card game to a sudden halt. "A number of complaints have been received from the tenants", he announced with all the authority he could muster. "In future, when referring to tenants don't refer to them as 'the fat oul one', 'the skinny oul one' or 'the little oul one', they should be addressed as the tenant in No. 10, 25 or whatever the house number is".

"For Christ's sake Christy, will you cop yourself on", replied one Alfie Carr out of the side of his mouth.

"I don't want to involve the Inspector", answered Christy.

"Maybe we should refer to them as lady of the house", suggested Alfie with a glint in his eye. "Some of the oul ones, I mean the tenants, are not what you could call ladies".

"Trust you to come up with something like that", said Christy, in an effort to impose his authority. "No more reference to the size or shape of the tenants, do youse hear".

"Not even if she is up the pole", retorted Alfie, warming to the debate. "You could hardly blame us for that, we are only here a few weeks". He laughed so much his oversized false teeth almost fell out of his mouth. "We will have none of that kind of talk on my job", warned Christy. "An oul fella like you should be saying your prayers, not passing insulting remarks like that".

"Christy, will you stop for Christ's sake, making a fool of yourself", replied Alfie, still struggling with his dentures.

It would be difficult to find a more contrary man than Alfie, always had something to complain about and liked nothing better than a good argument. A small, stocky middle-aged man with a pronounced limp, that forced him to utilise his trusty moped to get around from job to job. Always the first to show on the street, the familiar sound of his moped starting up signalled tea or lunch break. His sharp, acidic tongue he reserved for anyone he considered to be working too diligently with taunts like, 'Hey, Ate the Work' or 'You'll be kept' as he sailed by on his faithful moped.

He was the bane of many a Foreman's life, especially an over zealous one, never missing an opportunity to remind the Foreman of where he came from and just as important, where he was going. He had a filthy habit when laughing of rattling his over-sized dentures with his tongue, causing them to rattle like hailstones on a glass roof.

Like many of his generation, horses were a passion, studying form comparing jockeys, owners and trainers. It added a little spice to an otherwise uneventful life. Could never pass a group of women in the street without passing some remark, he would have the woman of the house in stitches with his sayings.

The whistle sounded like reveille, sending a reluctant crew back to work, leaving Archie to clean up the mess, Dave and John resumed work on the door. During the course of the afternoon progress was made on the door, in spite of the fact that the repairs such as cutting tenons, morticing and moulding had to be carried out by hand. By late afternoon the door was reassembled and glued together, leaving it ready for re-hanging next morning.

At 4.45 it was time to gather up tools, placing them in the safety of the hut. The crew arrived in plenty of time, lead by the ever ready Alfie astride his moped, much to the annoyance of the Foreman, forever fearful of the Inspector's arrival, placing his position in jeopardy.

The following morning the crew assembled inside the crowded hut in anticipation of the 8.30 deadline, with smoke everywhere. One old carpenter, Jem

Lowe, a small delicate grey haired man with a few fingers missing from his right hand, the result of an accident with an electric saw, lit up.

No sooner did he take a drag from the cigarette than the coughing commenced. It raked through his frail body from his toes to the top of his grey hair. Bent in two like a book his face turned a light shade of blue as the smoke penetrated his long suffering lungs. It was a daily performance, only this time it went deeper, causing even hardened smokers to cringe in despair.

"Oh, for God's sake, Jem, will you stop smoking before you give yourself a heart attack", cried Alfie, himself a non-smoker. Jem was unable to reply, just a feeble wave of his gammy hand.

"Will someone put him outside before he drops dead", insisted Alfie reflecting the views of those present. "It would turn your stomach listening to that".

Two young carpenters who could not endure this disgusting spectacle any longer, gently but firmly lifted a protesting Jem outside where he continued his smoke-induced recital. Even after the whistle had blown for roll call he was unable to reply.

The day commenced with each man in his turn discussing the work in progress with the Foreman, who issued a new docket if required before departing to his respective places of work. It was quite normal to spend a few days in the one house, if the amount of work was justified.

"Alfie, how are you fixed for work", enquired Christy.

"I'm ok.", replied Alfie.

"You sure, that's the third day in that house", insisted Christy.

"Christy, I worked when there was no work, for McAlpine on the Hills Stanleymore, where the well hangs on the bush and they put pigs head in the wall to watch the band go by".

"McAlpine, you must be joking", interjected Jim Burke the Shop Steward". "They wouldn't let you look in the gate at the others working never mind give you a job".

"Jealously will get you nowhere", laughed Alfie. "Yo-de-le-hee-dee", as he sauntered out the door, rocking from side to side with his gammy leg, like a well oiled sailor.

Dave organised the delivery of the repaired door with Archie and made his way in the company of another young Carpenter, John Drennan, who turned out to be quite a character. Having joined the B.A. at an early age, probably giving the wrong age, he saw service in many of the troubled parts of the world, Aden, Cyprus and Egypt. His arms were covered in colourful and bizarre tattoos, the exaggerated stories of foreign women certainly raised a few eyebrows among the younger men but shocked the older men not accustomed to such graphic and explicit detail.

It so happened they were detailed to work in adjoining houses, Dave to re-hang the door and John to fit a few new sashes. In the course of removing a defective sash, John somehow managed to give himself a cut on the hand with a gouge, a chisel-like tool rarely used on maintenance work. There was blood all over the kitchen sink and on the floor, when the woman of the house saw the blood drenched sink she nearly passed out, urging him to take himself off to the nearest hospital for treatment.

"It's nothing, Missus, just a flesh wound", said John running his injured hand under the cold tap.

The mixing of blood and water only increased the woman's fears as the bloody mixture swirled down the sink like a wash-down Abattoir.

She recoiled in horror at the mess. John, unperturbed, requested a needle and thread.

"What are you want a needle and thread for", said the woman, with a look of horror on her face.

"To stitch the wound of course", he answered, "if you have white thread all the better".

The woman, visibly shaken at what he proposed to do, quietly slipped out of the kitchen and returned with the necessary needle and thread. He thanked her, then sat down at the kitchen table and proceeded to sew up the wound. This proved too much for the woman; she took her leave and ran to tell her next door neighbour. When finished, calmly he wrapped his hand in a handkerchief and returned to whatever work he was doing.

The loud crackling of Alfie's moped firing off reminded all that it was time for hot drinks, so along with the others, Dave put away his tools and followed the gang in the direction of the hut. Word of John's altercation with the gouge preceded him, the women's network moved faster than sound; his colleagues viewed him with both horror and admiration. Some considered him a head-case, a victim of his army service, others thought he had some nerve 'must have picked up a trick or two in his travels'. The handkerchief was removed a few days later with hardly a mark to show for his trouble, from that day forward his was only known as 'Stitch'.

John and Dave were quickly assimilated into the gang; by the very nature of their work building workers are an itinerant breed, moving from job to job as a way of life. Long term friendships are rare, there is no point in getting to close to someone, knowing that at a moments' notice you can be transferred or sacked, destined never to meet again, all one can do is enjoy the moment. This transient lifestyle forced you to fit into any position, to work with a variety of people, it created an independent streak, making only short-term friendships, before moving on to the next job. "Bumped into Lesso the other day" said Jim Burke the shop steward, during a quiet moment one lunch-hour. "He had a bit of bad luck'. 'Don't tell me his mot is gone again", enquired the ever-present Alfie.

"No, nothing like that", answered Jim, "do you never think of anything else".

"At my age that's all I can do, is think about it", replied Alfie. "What happened anyway".

"He was working in Joseph's Place, you know, up off Dorset Street, laying a new floor" say Jim. "There was three small children in the house and you know how small those houses are".

"Yes, indeed, two rooms and a scullery out the back", Alfie replied.

"Anyway, he had to move the furniture out of the bedroom into the living-room before he could start", replied Jim. "Later that day, when the floor was finished, he had to put the furniture back on his own".

"Should have had a mate with him", interjected Alfie.

"Be that as it may", said Jim, "at half-four it was pitch dark outside and the rain was pouring down, so he took a chance and slipped away early".

"First rule – never leave your post before your time", Alfie nodded wisely.

"What was he supposed to do", cried Jim, "the job was finished, the woman of the house was trying to prepare the dinner and he was in the way".

"Just the same, he should have waited", replied Alfie, noted for his strict adherence to time-keeping.

"He jumped on a bus in Blessington Street and him being a non-smoker went inside and sat down", continued Jim, having grabbed everyone's attention, gossip from any source was feasted upon, "as you know his sight is not the best".

"Refuses to wear glasses", Alfie reminded all present, "thinks it might spoil his appearance".

"Will you let the man tell the story", interrupted a voice from across the table, "we haven't got all day".

"You'll never guess who he sat down beside?", asked Jim.

"His Granny", retorted Alfie, annoyed at being accused of interfering with the telling of the story.

"The Inspector", announced Jim to a hushed gathering.

"Holy Jaysus, how unlucky can you get", said a surprised Alfie.

"And where do you think you are going this hour of the day", asks your man. "Mind your own effin business", snorted Lesso, not realising who it was he was talking to, when he turned around and saw who it was he nearly shit in his trousers.

"So would you", said Alfie, nodding his head in disbelief, "what happened?".

"You can imagine, 'hungry-head' threw the book at him", replied an angry Jim.

"What I'd like to know", enquired Alfie, "what was your man doing on a bus, he is supplied with a staff car".

"It appears that the car was in for servicing", answered Jim. "If only he had of went upstairs, he would have got away with it".

"Lesso refuses to wear glasses; thinks it will spoil his appearance". "That bastard would hang his own Mother, that's if he ever had a Mother in the first place", snapped Alfie, expressing the feelings of those present. "He will die roaring".

"I was thinking of having a collection next pay day", said Jim, searching the faces for approval, "next time it could be one of us, any objections".

A request like this, coming from the Shop Steward was accepted without dissent.

Jim had been elected Shop Steward by the crew, mostly because no-one else wanted it. He undertook his task with vigour and attention. Many's the lunch hour, (actually a half-hour), was taken up with speeches extolling the virtues of the Union, with many interruptions from a good humoured crew, as he laid it on the line the changes to restore the dignity of the working man.

A passionate interest in the Republican movement is best illustrated by his practical commitment to the restoration of Kilmainham Jail. Working and organising a crew of his fellow work mates to work for nothing over a number of years when it was in a derelict state and not very fashionable, was his way of giving expression to the cause.

Thankfully the weather remained fine, enabling John and Dave to work outside, where the work continued apace, the door repairs soon petered out leaving them to concentrate their efforts on repairs to sashes.

The repair work to sashes was just as skilful but less demanding. The same procedure was adopted, a plywood sheet replaced the defective sash, and it was then repaired and re-hung. On one of these sorties to retrieve a defective sash, Dave could not help but observe a young Carpenter, Paddy Clinch, not renowned for his finesse or skill, working in an adjoining house. He was in the process of replacing a defective fixed sash to the kitchen window. Clearly he overheard the woman of the house implore him to try and save the glass in the window.

"Don't worry, Missus, you are in safe hands", he said, "nothing to worry about".

"My husband bought and fitted that glass himself", she stated, "it cost him a right few bob".

He set about removing the sash from the inside, using a large nail bar to lever it out. There was much noisy hammering as he tried to save the glass. Slowly, gently the sash began to loosen, with the aid of a hacksaw he managed to cut the nails holding the sash in place, the woman hovered in the background, her hands crossed in prayer. With one final effort it came free, the glass intact.

Placing the pane of broad-reeded glass in a vertical position against the wall, he called in triumph to the woman.

"Missus, I've saved the glass".

The woman blessed herself and sighed with relief, quickly she made her way to the yard, just in time to see the pane of glass slowly, gently, crash into a thousand pieces. He had, of course, left the glass bolt upright, the slightest movement of wind done the rest.

The attitude of the tenants to the imposition of a gang of Corporation workers that descended on them like a swarm of locust was always positive. In spite of the disruption it caused they were made welcome. It was always the woman of the house that welcomed them, the curtains were taken down, space was made, furniture moved to facilitate the work. Their wholehearted acceptance certainly made life more tolerable; they were invited into the home and given the freedom of the house, even to the extent of a key to the hall door. In some cases the work could extend to over three or four days. At no time were they ever made feel unwelcome, cups of tea were the order of the day. Occasionally one came across a less than clean house, (referred to as a Gonk); families in difficult circumstances, the welcome never varied. In such cases the quicker the work was finished the better for yourself. One of the less desirable aspects was to witness children suffering as a result of poverty, not of their own making.

With such a wide and diverse gathering, some real weird characters stood out; one in particular went under the title of 'The Rat Hogan'. If ever a name was suitably appropriate, it described him perfectly. A miserable, obnoxious, narrow-faced man with a pointed nose, forever in need of cleaning, over which hung a dirty, shiny flat cap. His ancient and equally shiny gabardine coat, at least four sizes too large for him, reaching to his heels, giving the appearance of a waterproof tent with feet.

He would put in an appearance each morning, collect his days' work and that was the last one saw of him till signing off time. Lunch he would scrounge from the tenant, much to the disgust of the other men, who, quite rightly perceived that this practice reflected badly on them. Being an old I.R.A. man each year at the annual commemoration ceremony he would march bedecked with medals with his former comrades behind the band to Arbour Hill. If he was an example of what had fought for Irish independence, the English could not have been up to much.

Eventually John and Dave found themselves joining the others affecting repairs to houses. It took time to adjust to working in the same house for a few days, especially with children ever present.

Carpenters tools to be effective have to be sharp. In the wrong hands a saw or a wood chisel can be a lethal weapon. Great care had to be exercised to ensure that inquisitive children, not realising the danger, did not get their hands on any tools. Having to lock away tools every time after their use, is time consuming and a nuisance, safer to insist that the children be restrained.

A heated debate arose between two carpenters, Jem Traynor and Peter O'Brien, over the use of a screwdriver. It was no ordinary screwdriver, a pump-screwdriver that Peter had bought while working in England. Jem took exception to its use, saying it gave an unfair advantage to Peter. As a result, a meeting was called during lunch-hour by the Shop Steward to discuss the matter.

"Brothers, I declare this meeting open, as you are well aware there has been a complaint from Brother Traynor concerning the use of a pump-screwdriver by one of our Brothers, Peter".

"That's right", stated Jem, "how are we expected to compete with a yoke like that".

"Hold on there", said Jim Burke, the Shop Steward, raising his voice to assert his authority, "you say that by him using a pump-screwdriver it affects you, how do you make that out".

"Of course it affects me", cried Jem, "that gadget drives screws like a machine, it is also against the Union rules".

"Where did you get that from", answered Peter scornfully, "what are you afraid of".

"Did you hear that", Jem appealed to the Shop Steward, "you won't always be so young".

"If I was your age I'd be at home in a rocking chair", retorted Peter, "what are you worried about, we are not on piecework".

"You'll get no medals from the Corporation, I can tell you that", said Jem, looking around for support.

"You can't hold back progress", insisted Peter, "we are in the 20th Century now, in case you haven't noticed".

"There won't be an hours work in this town unless someone makes a stand", replied a man not given to argument.

"I'm not sure if it is against the Union rules or not", said an undecided Jim, "in my opinion it's not".

"Let's have a ballot", cried Jem, hoping to achieve a victory by appealing to the others, "see what the majority thinks".

"You better make it quick", interrupted Christy. "I'll be blowing the whistle in about 5 minutes".

"All right, all right", shouted Jim, "we have a motion to put before you, 'that the use of a pump screwdriver be discontinued', who will second the motion". "Right the motion is seconded by Charlie. Due to the fact that time is of the essence we will have to dispense with a secret ballot, all in favour raise their right hand, and I don't want anyone voting twice, do you hear".

The hands were raised, the numbers counted and a second ballot was called amid much good-humoured banter by all concerned. The numbers were again counted and the result was a draw, 15 each, with no casting vote, stalemate.

"What do we do now", asked Peter, "am I to use it or not?"

"I'll have to consult the Union delegate and get a ruling from him", Jim informed the crew. "In the meantime refrain from using the pump-screwdriver".

"How long will that take?", enquired Jem, anxious to have the situation resolved.

"I'll let you know as soon as I find out", replied Jim.

The whistle blew, bringing an end to a silly debate; the use or non-use of a pump-screwdriver was of little interest. It was seen as a diversion that livened up lunch-hour. The Shop Steward is obliged to discuss any complaint he received, no matter how trivial, and to take whatever action he considered necessary.

The arrival of a lorry laden down with the makings of a Hut heralded the imminent arrival of the Painters. The lorry was unloaded and a number of Carpenters were detailed to assemble the Hut. It also signalled that the Carpenters' work was coming to a close, inducing a sense of fear and anxiety amongst the older and mostly temporary staff. Would this be the end of the road, the last hurrah for many of them?

There was a lot of speculation and debate as to what was to be the next job, if any. Some were resigned to the fact that they were finished. The Painters duly appeared in their white suite, that certainly added a little colour to the otherwise drab surroundings. An air of expectant gloom settled on the Carpenters Hut, each day was a bonus, till eventually the word came. The job was finished, the crew or what was left of it transferred to other jobs, the worse fears of the older men was confirmed, they were to be let go.

The fateful day arrived. The list was posted revealing the full extent of the proposed lay-offs, no redundancy payments for them, just a weeks' notice. All their working lives they had to contend with lay-offs, no matter how many times it had occurred over the years it still hurt.

In spite of a lifetime of casual work behind them, there was something rather poignant at the sight of a group of tradesmen closing their toolboxes for the last. Knowing this was inevitable but preferring to dismiss it, refusing to admit that they were no longer required, who wanted 60 and 70 year old men.

Best of luck exchanges were made, plans to keep in touch were sincerely offered, it still could not conceal the sadness at the passing of that generation.

They knew and understood it was to be the last time they would ever lunch together, swap sandwiches and stories and laugh at the follies of life. For a short space in time it had bonded them together, even if they were unaware of it. The 'Billy Cans', so often the cause of dispute over ownership, were laid to rest, no more complaints of smoking water spoiling the taste of tea.

The Foreman, Christy, without a word of thanks, found himself 'back on his tools', relegated and humiliated, not knowing what kind of reception to expect from his former subordinates. Even the bold Archie, for once in his life, was at a loss for something to say. He too was to be laid off. With warm handshakes John and Dave reluctantly parted company and went their separate ways. Dave returned to the 'Zone' in the North Strand and John went to another 'Paint Job' in Ballyfermot. They were destined never to meet again.

St. Brigids Gardens, Mayor Street Upper

On the Zone

The following morning I arrived on my bike at the Depot in the North Strand to be confronted by a large gathering of men, of all shapes and sizes, waiting to present themselves like "button men" on the Quays. I checked in with the "Timekeeper" and joined the waiting crowd. As the clock approached 8.30 a.m. the pace of new arrivals increased considerably, five minutes grace was permitted after which the ever present timekeeper removed all cards. Those arriving late were docked a half-hour's pay, persistent latecomers were subjected to a rigorous punishment, suspension or in extreme cases, dismissal was the order of the day.

A long, narrow passageway with hatches on one side and the Stores on the other, depending on the weather, was usually crowded with a mixture of tradesmen, representing all of the building trades. Each man in his turn presented himself at one of the hatches to give an account of his previous day's efforts to a Foreman. Many's a heated discussion took place between Foreman and tradesman, each claiming, in their turn, that they had or had not fulfilled their contract.

New works orders were issued. One never knew what to expect in the way of work. It could be anything from fitting a new door, laying a floor, replacing sash cords to renewing a toilet seat, the list was endless. This presented some difficulties when it came to tools. A box of carpenter's tools can be a problem, especially trying to get from job to job under your own steam. Most used a bicycle; having a car was light years away. Other tradesmen had a helper to do the necessary for them.

"Porky Welsh, you're next for shaving", shouted Paddy Boylan, one of the Foremen over the heads of the crowd.

The rather large figure of 'Porky' emerged from the pack and leaned against the hatch.

"What have you been up to now?", enquired the Foreman.

"Me? I'm as innocent as a new born baby", came 'Porky's' reply.

"Yeah, sure you are, and I'm Charles Stewart Parnell", said the Foreman.

"Any relation to yer man with his arm out in O'Connell Street?" Porky answered sharply.

"Never mind the wise cracks", the Foreman replied. "I only hope you have a good story ready for your man".

"The old dog for the hard road", was Porky's response.

Porky was indestructible. He was also the archetypal "Irishman"; a loveable rogue imbued with a terrible thirst that required a constant supply of liquid replenishment. Noted for his complete disregard of authority, this manifested itself in his many close encounters with that same authority, most notably his "Nemesis", the Inspector. He had, on so many occasions, been caught off the job, sneaking off early and many other similar offences, but somehow he had always managed to save his skin.

A big stout man, his rather large tummy held in place by a well worn gabardine coat, the buttons of which were strained to their limits, the belt had long since become redundant. A soft hat that appeared to be glued in place, never to reveal if he was bald or not, overhung his red shiny face, particularly on a Monday morning. Not noted for his finesse at his trade, a carpenter, he nevertheless managed to get by, mostly on his wits. Constantly on the move from job to job, like an itinerant, his reputation always preceded him. No sooner had he settled on one job than he was shifted to another. No one wished to be the one who finally shafted him.

The Inspector, as was his want, cruised the area late every day, perhaps hoping to catch someone off their job when, who did he see, only the redoubtable 'Porky' cycling along with four lengths of flooring boards strapped to his bike.

"I've got him now", he cried to himself as he returned to the Depot to check the details, "this is the end of the road for 'Porky'".

"Knock, Knock".

"Come in", came the reply.

"You wanted to see me, Mr. MacDonagh?" asked 'Porky', walking into the small office with an innocent look on his face; all that was missing was a halo.

"I certainly do", answered the Inspector firmly, without raising his head. "Tell me, did you or did you not have a flooring job to do in Carnlough Road yesterday".

"Yes, I did, why?" enquired 'Porky' carefully, "is something wrong?"

"And did you do it?" said Mr. MacDonagh, slowly raising his eyes to confront 'Porky'.

"Well you see, there was a little problem with that job", ventured 'Porky'.

"Is that so?" replied the Inspector, staring right through 'Porky'. "I just happened to be passing that way yesterday evening and I saw you making tracks with a few lengths of flooring tied to your bike, can you explain that, please?"

"It was like this Mr. MacDonagh", came the reply. "I didn't have enough time to start the job so I decided to take it home with me, all in the interest of security, you understand".

"If you expect me to believe that you have another think coming", answered the Inspector in disbelief. "I've heard some good stories in my time, but this one takes the prize".

"It's the truth, I swear on my Mother's grave", 'Porky' said, shifting his not inconsiderable weight from foot to foot, "the tenant refused to accept responsibility for the flooring overnight".

"Pull the other leg, it's got bells on it", snapped the Inspector impatiently. "I have over the years tried to overlook your shortcomings, but stealing materials, this time you have gone too far".

"Honest to God", implored 'Porky', "go and see for yourself".

"Don't worry, I intend to, right away", the Inspector said, convinced he had finally nailed 'Porky', "get back to your work, before I have you charged with theft".

"Yes sir", answered 'Porky', retreating to the safety of the open yard.

Within the hour the Inspector checked out the story and, much to his surprise and disappointment, the flooring was in the house. "The cute whore must have got a whisper", he thought to himself.

That very evening, at exactly 4 o'clock, 'Porky' was detailed to report to Upper Ballyfermot … the equivalent of Outer Mongolia, as far removed from the City Centre as it was possible to get. What the Inspector failed to understand was that there was 4/6 (27p) per day travelling time on that job, with wages at £10.00 per week. The extra money was like a pay rise, not bad for one supposed to be punished. The final irony, where did 'Porky' live, where else but Ballyfermot?

Some years later, even on his deathbed, when visited by one of his workmates, his last words were, and I quote, "Don't tell the Inspector you saw me". A fitting epitaph.

"'Nigger' Hourahan" came the call from the Foreman's office. A hush descended on the crowd as a figure emerged from the crowded passageway, elbowing his way to the open hatch. A small, stocky man of indeterminate age, with a very sallow complexion, hence the nickname, but it was his eyes that were his most striking feature. They were deep, penetrating, fierce, like two holes burned in a blanket. The heavy bags under his eyes were like a pair of wet socks hanging from a clothesline. The 'Nigger' was considered a hard man, not one to cross, renowned for his quick temper and sharp tongue; he came from a long line of bricklayers.

He leaned into the open hatch to confront the Foreman, the smell from his breath forced Harry Buckley to retreat out of range.

"Harry, give me something handy this morning", growled the 'Nigger', "me poor head is in a terrible state".

"I can see that", replied Harry, still keeping his distance.

By contrast, Harry was a kind, nervous man, almost timid in his approach to staff, a fine carpenter in his day, but when it came to exercising authority he had never been known to discipline anyone regardless of what they may have done. An interesting man, unusual in that he played a fine piano, and after a few drinks had been known to do a creditable soft shoe shuffle.

"Here's a few cheek blocks for Mary's Mansions, that should keep you busy for a while", said Harry, "see you tomorrow", happy to see the back of the 'Nigger'.

"Thanks Harry, you just saved a life", replied the 'Nigger' as he turned away, handing the works order to his mate 'Ryco'. "Here, give that to Martin in the Stores, then go and tell the oul one in 35 we are coming to fit cheek blocks".

"What if the fire is lighting, it's very cold this morning", answered 'Ryco'.

"That's her tough luck", came the sharp reply, "she will just have to put it out. How are we supposed to fit new cheek blocks with the fire lighting". With that he turned away and out the gates, heading, no doubt, for the nearest 7 o'clock house.

I presented myself at the hatch, wondering what to expect in the way of work.

"Ah, a new face, welcome, we'll see what you are made of", said Paddy Boylan. "Charlie Keegan", he shouted over my shoulder. We were joined by a tall rangy man from the West, Leitrim I think, no introduction was made. "I want the pair of youse to replace a floor in a house just opposite here, here's the works order".

Charlie turned out to be a warm, friendly man, easy to work with, a fine Irish fiddler in his spare time.

"The first thing to do is to go and tell the woman of the house what we are going to do", said Charlie in his soft country accent.

We went immediately to the house to inform the woman. She expressed surprise.

"Holy God, you mean now, this morning", she said in a concerned voice, "it's months since I report that, I thought you had forgotten".

"We only got it this morning, Ma'am", I replied.

"But I have to get the children out for school", she implored, "can you give me a little time?"

"Certainly Ma'am, we have to arrange for the timber to be delivered", Charlie replied, "and don't worry about the furniture, we'll take care of that".

"Thanks".

By contrast, Paddy Boylan was loud, gruff, noisy, much given to shouting, especially when trying to get staff out of the Depot each morning; a tall, red-faced man in his middle years, with heavy horn rimmed glasses, behind which hid a wicked sense of humour. There were times when some of the staff would try his patience to the limit. If you had to be reprimanded you got it straight between the eyes, in public, in front of everyone. But that would be the end of it, it went no further, for which he was much respected. In his case his bark was certainly worse than his bite.

The following weeks were, to say the least, interesting. The maintenance work carried out was basic, replacing locks, doors, sashes but it was the working conditions, where some of the places one was obliged to work were simply appalling. After a while one became immune to smells, D.D.T. became part of your everyday tool kit.

Arriving early one morning, normally a crowd gathered outside the Depot, talking horses or football, there wasn't a soul in sight; even the large sliding doors were closed. Parking the bike, Dave slipped in the side door, only to find the passageway jam-packed with bodies. Along with the smoke an air of expectancy filled the place.

Paddy Boylan came out of the office and made his way through the crowd in the direction of the closed sliding doors.

"Peter, any sign?" he enquired.

"Nothing doing so far", came Peter's reply as he withdrew his head from an opening in the doors.

"Try again, will you", insisted Boylan.

"What's going on?" Dave asked Charlie.

"Don't you know?" replied Charlie, "it's Andy Doyle".

"So, it's Andy Doyle", Dave answered, still at a loss to know what was going on, "what's he done, won the Sweep or what".

"Quiet", shouted Boylan, as he glared at the restless crowd, "Peter, any use?"

"Yes, he's coming", said Peter, drawing in his head from a gap in the door.

"The next one to make a sound gets shifted to the Dangerous Buildings", stated Boylan emphatically.

Down the street came the redoubtable Andy, on his upstairs model bike, unaware what was going on. He was a quiet, harmless, inoffensive elderly man, a widower with a grown family who had married a widow the previous year, who in turn had a family of her own. No sooner had he dismounted than the doors burst open and out charged the mob.

A bewildered Andy found himself swept off his feet and hoisted on to strong shoulders that then proceeded to march him up and down the narrow street amid cries of "Good oul Andy" and "True for ya". Poor mortified Andy was then deposited, feet first, before Paddy Boylan, who grabbed his hand, declaring loudly, "I never thought you had it in you".

"It was nothing really, Paddy", replied an embarrassed Andy.

"Are you kidding?" answered Paddy, "it's not every day one gets a chance to shake the hand of a man whose wife has just presented him with triplets!"

"All right, you've had your bit of fun", cried Paddy.

"So has Andy", came the quick reply, "and I bet he's sorry".

"If you are not all out of here in 2 minutes, I'll start docking time", shouted Paddy, "Get them lorries out of here".

The Lodging House, Benburb Street.

Benburb Street

I t was one of those cold February mornings; everyone wrapped in heavy clothes, woollen hats and scarves of many colours very much in evidence. Inside the Depot the sound of feet stamping on the even colder concrete floor in an effort to keep the circulation going. There was much blowing of hands, the white breath mixed with cigarette smoke rising slowly, dissipating on making contact with the asbestos roof.

"Not many brass monkeys out this morning", someone said.

"Would you blame them", came the reply. "They have more sense than us".

"Hope I get an inside job", said Dave, one of the gang, waiting for the hatch to open.

His name was called along with another Carpenter, Jimmy Dempsey. They presented themselves at the open hatch.

"Have you both got a hammer and a nail punch with youse?", asked the Foreman.

"Of course we have", they both replied.

"Good, I want both of you to go to the Lodging House in Benburb Street, right away".

"The Lodging House!", said a shocked Jimmy, "you must be joking".

"On the first floor dormitory where the men sleep I want every nail in the floor punched down", answered the Foreman with a mischievous glint in his eye.

"Ah for God's sake Paddy, that place is full of fleas, bugs and God only knows what", replied a still shocked Jimmy.

"I'm sorry, but one of the old lodgers tore his foot on a nail, so every nail has to be punched down", said Paddy. "And don't miss any or you are both in trouble".

"I know who I'd like to punch", mumbled Dave under his breath. "What's that you said?", enquired Paddy, ignoring the remark. It gave him no pleasure to send anyone to the Lodging House but someone had to go. "By the way, don't forget to bring some D.D.T. with you, just in case".

They were an interesting and contrasting pair, having worked together occasionally. Dave on the one hand was tall, skinny, single and easy-going who enjoyed playing football at weekends. During the week his spare time was taken up with playing music, whether practising his trumpet or performing with the Concert Band.

Jimmy, on the other hand, was middle-aged, small and stocky in stature, with a dark swarthy complexion, always in need of a shave known as 'The Strangler', his very long arms were out of proportion to his short arms.

He was unusual in that him being a city person he spoke fluent Irish, never missed an opportunity to speak 'Cupla Focal', much to the annoyance of the Foreman who perceived, quite rightly, that he was making fun of them. Even though married he devoted any of his spare time to the running of a boys' club in the Coombe area of the city where he lived.

After much grumbling they gathered their tools, secured them to their bikes and in the company of Billy Sheperd the Plumber and his mate Joe they reluctantly headed off.

"Where are you going Billy?", asked Dave.

"To Benburb Street Flats", replied Billy, "a choke in one of the flats". We've been stuck with the Lodging House, what a dump", Jimmy said as they made their way up Parnell Street in the direction of the Markets. "Where are we going to get a cup of tea; don't fancy the Lodging House".

"I'd sooner do without it than in that kip of a place", retorted Dave, not impressed with this assignment.

"There's a place in Greek Street Flats", answered Billy. "The Caretaker is a decent oul skin; just as important, the place is clean".

"That's more than I can say for some of the Caretakers", replied Dave.

"It's so clean you could eat off the floor", said Billy.

As there were no canteen facilities provided for the staff they were left to depend on the generosity of the tenants and Caretakers to boil a can of water. One was obliged to cultivate an understanding with Caretakers for the basics, with only a half-hour lunch-break. There was no possibility of making for home except for those lucky enough to live nearby. The humble bicycle was the most common form of transport, it is no joke to try and carry a box of tools a distance without the aid of a bike, a car was unheard of.

Billy was a small, sallow-faced man, never ever seen without his heavy brown overcoat, Winter or summer, always the overcoat. His work-mates believed that without his overcoat Billy would cease to exist. The pince-nez glasses he wore gave him a sort of eastern look, hence the nickname, 'Mr. Moto', his squeaky voice didn't help either.

In contrast his mate Joe was a huge burly young man with a flat nose, the result of his efforts in the boxing arena. Known as the 'Horizontal Heavyweight', it was said of him that he knew every crack in the ceiling of the National Boxing Stadium having finished most of his fights on the flat of his back.

Not renowned for his speed of thought it was comical to see the pair of them together, Joe towering over his mate and Billy laying down the law on how the work should be done.

Entering the gates of the flats to be greeted by the Caretaker.

"Billy, the right man in the right place", he said cheerfully.

"Don't tell me, another one of your tenants in trouble", answered Billy, his narrow eyes squinting through his glasses.

"How did you guess", replied the Caretaker, "there is a leaking tap in one of the flats, can you do anything to help".

"I don't know. Without a docket it's risky", said Billy. "If I get caught doing a nixer, I'll be sacked, you know that".

"I know, I know, but she is a decent woman, never complains", answered the Caretaker. "Has a stall in Moore Street".

"Tell you what", said Billy, "send in a report with the Timekeeper when he calls, it will cover me".

"That's great, would you fancy a cup of tea?", he enquired.

"If you insist", Billy said quickly.

"Thought youse would never ask", interjected Jimmy.

"My mother always said that there is nothing like a cup of 'scald' to warm your heart", replied Billy with a dry laugh.

The caretaker had a 'dug-out', a room under the stairs where he stored brushes, disinfectants, shovels, etc. It was laid out with a bench seat and a small table, a large aluminium kettle was sitting on a gas ring, almost on the boil. Each in their turn handed in their mixed tea and sugar and in no time the tea was ready.

It was with relish they enjoyed their tea break of sandwiches, washed down with plenty of warm tea, just the job on such a cold morning.

"Come on Jimmy, we better get moving", said Dave. "I'm not exactly looking forward to this job, the quicker we start, the quicker we finish".

"I couldn't agree more, even if it means working through lunch-hour", replied Jimmy, "it's going to be a lousy job, no matter which way you look at it".

Leaving their bikes in the safety of the 'dug-out' and thanking the Caretaker, they crossed Smithfield and in to Benburb Street.

"See you later", said Billy stopping at the entrance to the flats, "this is where I get off".

"Don't do anything we wouldn't do", answered Jimmy.

"In a kip like this, you must be joking", replied Billy as he disappeared into the dark hallway.

Dave and Jimmy passed some of the old "Dossers" leaving the Lodging House and a sad pitiful sight they were too. broken men left to wander the streets for the rest of the day, Winter and summer, in all weathers, having been turned out on to the street, unable to return to the refuge till later that day.

"So, this is the famous 'Lodging House'", announced Dave as they stood on the footpath outside a five-storey red-bricked building as the last of the residents ventured out into the cold morning air. Gingerly they entered the hallway, not knowing what to expect, so many stories had been told over the years of the conditions that existed, especially the dormitories. On the right hand side was a sort of rest room, with chairs, tables and a radio staring out from a high shelf in the centre of the room.

They were met by the Porter who enquired, "Sorry lads, you are too late, call back later and we will see what we can do for you".

"We are not looking for accommodation", cried Jimmy, "we are two Carpenters to fix the floors".

"Hope we are never reduced to that", interjected Dave.

"Sorry about that", replied the Porter, "we get all sorts of in here you know, follow me". He lead the way up the concrete stairs to the first floor landing, into a large dormitory at the front of the building.

The dormitory was divided into a series of cubicles, each containing a bed, a chair and a locker with a curtain to form a door. The place reeked with the combined smells of unwashed bodies, clothes, cigarettes and many other unmentionable smells.

They made straight for the windows to let in some badly needed fresh air, the freezing air rushed in, it was preferable to the disgusting state of the dormitory.

"One of the oul fellas tore his foot on a nail yesterday", said the Porter, pointing to the head of a nail protruding above the surface of the flooring-board, "you should have seen the blood, it was everywhere".

"We will take your word for it", replied Dave feeling very uncomfortable in these surroundings, "what about the cubicles, you can't really expect us to get on our hands and knees in there".

"The Inspector said every nail was to be punched down", answered the Porter. "It's up to yourselves what you do if another one tears his foot, don't blame me".

"Jimmy, do you see the conditions of the cubicles", cried an alarmed Dave, "they are manky".

"I'm just as appalled as you", said Jimmy, "the sooner we get finished the better, there's nothing for it only down on our knees and start punching nails as fast as we can".

"By the way, I didn't bother to sweep out this morning", smiled the Porter. "Thought I'd wait till you are finished".

There are a lot of nails in a floor this size.

They tried to ignore anything that was on the floor, especially under the beds. Nevertheless it was most distasteful work. Working on building sites was oft times dirty but at least it could be brushed off. As there was very little work available in the building trade one could not pick and choose the type of work preferred. Most tradesmen of their generation were either idle or in England so you made the most of your lot, although with this kind of work, they often wondered.

Billy and his mate made their way up the dark stairs to the top floor. Arriving breathless Billy was obliged to lean against the wall to recover his wind, Joe never even noticed. The toilet block was situated to the rear of the building, a sign on the wall indicated Male and Female. Each of the pans were full to the brim, some overflowed on to the floor, the smell was dreadful. Back down the stairs to the yard and with the aid of a shovel borrowed from the Caretaker, Joe lifted the manhole cover to check. The manhole was clear, indicating that the soil-stack was the source of the problem.

"Oh no", cried Billy, "you know what this means".

"No, what?", answered a puzzled Joe.

"We are going to need a 60 foot ladder to get the choke away", replied Billy.

"Where are we going to get a 60 foot ladder from?", asked Joe.

"From the Depot, where else", Billy said, "you stay here and put the cover back on the manhole, I'm going to phone the Depot".

Away he went, scurrying across the street to a public telephone, returning quickly and looking decidedly uncomfortable, the prospect of having to scale a 60 foot ladder to relieve a choke was the last thing he needed.

They waited an hour in the freezing cold for the lorry to arrive. The next problem was to manhandle the ladder, section by section through the narrow hall, to an equally small yard. Between Joe and the lorry helper they somehow managed to get the bottom section into a vertical position, not without first getting tangled up in the many clothes lines stretched across the yard. Some of the language used in the process was colourful to say the least.

The other sections were hoisted into place with the aid of ropes, the top section straddling the soil-pipe for safety, the bottom was footed by the redouble Joe.

Billy stood looking up the ladder, his beady eyes almost closed as he contemplated his next move. He armed himself with spanners, screwdriver and a plunger before setting off up the ladder. He climbed slowly, clinging to the sides of the ladder for dear life as he inched his way, step by step. At the halfway stage the ladder began to sway in and out, causing him to panic, he wrapped himself around the ladder in an effort to stop the swaying. The swaying stopped momentarily giving him heart to go on. No sooner did he recommence his climb than the swaying began again.

"Are you all right Billy?", shouted Joe from the safety of the yard.

Ignoring the call he somehow crawled his way to the top and stopped beside the cleaning-eye on the soil stack. With one arm entwined in the rung of the ladder, not daring to look down, he reached, spanner in hand, to remove the cover. In spite of the cold, tiny beads of perspiration trickled down his face, brought on by fear. The spanner locked on to one of the two brass nuts that held the cover in place, he began to rewind it. Slowly, carefully, it loosened sufficiently for him to use his fingers in case the bolt fell to the ground.

As the last tread was released the bolt came free in his hand, suddenly the cleaning-door shot off into space.

The filthy contents of the blocked soil-stack spewed out all over the place, catching poor Billy front on, covering him with the remains of the choked drain as it poured out. Down below, on hearing Billy's cry, Joe, for once in his life, moved quickly, ducking as he ran to the safety of the back door before it all came pouring down into the yard. For a minute no one dared move until it exhausted itself. Joe peered out slowly, his eyes searching for the sad figure of Billy still hanging on for dear life, his clothes destroyed.

Billy was transfixed. If the climb up the ladder was an experience he wanted to forget, it was nothing compared with having to climb down a wet and slippy ladder. With courage, born out of fear and disgust, he began the dangerous descent, his feet squelching with each step he took.

The torturous journey proceeded without mishap. Arriving at the foot of the ladder Billy was in a distressed and exhausted state of mind and body. He stood in the centre of the yard looking down at his favourite brown overcoat that had taken the brunt of the discharge.

"What happened Billy?", asked Joe innocently, not realising the significance of what he had just witnessed. Still he made no effort to assist his mate.

"Are you blind as well as being punch-drunk", cried Billy with rage, "can't you see what happened?".

Joe just stared at the solitary figure of Billy standing there covered with the most foul and disgusting mess.

"Whoever was at the cleaning eye before me wrung the treads on one of the bolts", said a distracted Billy, "as soon as I removed the other bolt the cover flew off".

"Jaysus Billy, you are destroyed, look at your good coat", replied Joe, his eyes focussed the condition of his mates' clothes, "what are you going to do?".

"One thing, I won't be having lunch at the Shelbourne, that's for sure", answered Billy sarcastically. "Go and get the Caretaker, he might be able to lend me a pair of overalls, anything to get out of this filthy lot".

Still staring at the mess Joe went and returned with the Caretaker, who on seeing the state of Billy could not contain himself and burst out laughing. This only infuriated Billy, it was bad enough nearly getting killed and saturated without him being humiliated and laughed at well. He marched across the yard, slopping his way through the remains of the choked drain, his narrow eyes blazing.

"Don't come any closer", cried the Caretaker, with tears streaming down his face. "Stay where you are, I'll see what I can do", as he dashed out the hallway, leaving the evil-smelling Plumber, framed in the open doorway. He returned shortly afterwards with an old boiler suit and a pair of 'Wellington Boots', about four sizes too large for Billy.

"That's the best I can do", said the Caretaker, "might get you home without getting you arrested for indecent exposure".

"Very amusing", snapped Billy as he began the messy job of removing the overcoat and shoes.

"Will I get the hose, just to wash you down like", asked Joe, trying to offer assistance.

"Just hand me the boiler-suit and the boots, I'll manage", said a resigned Billy.

"The only disinfectant I have is 'Jeyes Fluid', said the Caretaker, "you are welcome to use it". Still keeping his distance he handed the suit and the boots to Joe. With a great deal of muttering and grumbling Billy somehow struggled into the suit, leaving his ruined clothes to be dumped in the rubbish bin.

"What about the dealer's leaking tap?", asked Joe.

"You know what you can do with that, I'm going home", replied Billy sharply.

Telling Joe to stay put he trundled out into the street, a sight to behold, with the large boiler suit and the oversized boots. His only thought was to get home as fast as possible and put this disastrous day behind him.

"I don't know which is worse", said Dave, "my back or my knees", as he straightened up seeking relief from the nail punching exercise.

"Thank God we are nearly finished", replied Jimmy, who kept hammering away, secure in the knowledge that this unpleasant and distasteful detail was almost complete.

"I wonder how did Billy get on", asked Dave.

"Billy is an old hand, he knows how to take care of himself", replied Jimmy.

"Do you want the pleasure of driving the last nail?", enquired Dave.

"I wouldn't dream of depriving you of that rather doubtful honour", answered Jimmy with a smile.

"Bang, bang, shag this place", replied Dave. "I never want to see the inside of this kip again, let's get out of here".

Gathering their tools and down the stairs only to be confronted in the entrance hall by the return of the homeless men, as they crowded in out of the cold. They each headed for the kitchen area on the ground floor with whatever food they had managed to beg, borrow or, in some cases, steal. A room set aside acted as a kitchen and was equipped with pots, pans, sinks, etc. and a number of gas rings for cooking food.

The air in the kitchen was consumed with steam, emanating from the many pots and pans that boiled furiously. The smells were many and varied, ranging from cabbage, potatoes, to fish and a variety of strange and exotic brews. It was a case of first in, first to cook; latecomers had to wait their turn, each guarded his food jealously not taking their eyes off the precious food for a second.

The centre of the room was filled with long tables for eating off; the food, when cooked, was quickly devoured.

"It's like something out of 'Dickens'", said Dave, visibly shocked, as they watched the unfortunate and tragic men trying to prepare whatever meagre food they had acquired.

"And we are complaining about the job we got", replied a sober voiced Jimmy, "at least we are assured of a meal and change of clothes when we get home; that's more than you can say for these poor souls".

It was a thoughtful and serious pair of Carpenters that headed back to the Caretaker's place to clean up, somehow or other, lunch did not seem very important.

Paint Job 1963.
A group of Painters with a lone Carpenter.

The Eviction

The following morning they received a right good slagging from the gang assembled outside the Depot, cries of 'here comes itch and scratch, the lousy joiners' rang out.

"Will youse lay off", replied Dave. "I had to change my clothes when I got home".

"That's what they all say", came the response as they began scratching themselves in unison. "You can get D.D.T. from Martin in the stores, he has loads of it in stock".

"One would think we were the first to have ever worked in the Lodging House", answered Jimmy.

"There's one sure thing, you didn't need a white apron", said Joe Reid, a long, skinny Plumber dressed in heavy overalls.

"Jealousy will get you nowhere", replied Jimmy.

"By the way, did you hear about Billy Sheppard?", enquired Joe.

"No, what happened?", asked Dave.

"Nearly bought it", said Joe.

"We were only down the street from him", replied Dave, "never heard a thing, we arranged to have lunch with him but we skipped it to get finished early".

Joe went on to explain the gory details and the consequences.

"You mean Billy's brown coat is no longer", said a shocked Dave. "How is he going to survive without it?".

"Must have been some operation to get that coat off", replied Jimmy. "I heard he even slept in it".

"Gone sick, won't be in for a few days", answered a concerned Joe.

"What was it that sickened him, the mess or the loss of the coat?", asked Dave.

"A little of both, I guess", said Joe.

A head appeared around the doorway of the Depot. "Boylan is in there roaring his head off looking for youse", stated the voice; "get in before he has a heart attack".

"Must have got a bad pint last night", said Jimmy.

As they made their way through the crowded passageway it became obvious that their exploits in the Lodging House had preceded them. The men recoiled in mock horror at their arrival, a great display of communal scratching was performed by all concerned.

"Well, how did you get on yesterday?", enquired Boylan with a grin as he moved back from the hatch.

"Jaysus, don't you start", cried Dave. "It's bad enough with that lot without you joining in".

"Just to show how generous I can be", said Boylan. "I put you both down for dirty money".

"You sure that the estimates can carry such a cost", replied Dave, "two shillings a day is a lot of money".

The type of work carried out varied from day to day, one never knew what to expect, sometimes it was fitting a new door, replacing window sashes, repairs to floors, the list is endless. The result of which, it was necessary to carry as wide a range of tools as possible to cover any eventuality. There is nothing worse than to find oneself stranded, trying to finish a job and short of something as basic as a hacksaw or a spanner. What do you do, ask the tenant, one can imagine the response. "Typical Corporation man, hasn't even got the tools to do the job".

"One thing before you go", said Boylan. "You are to meet the Sheriff this afternoon for an eviction".

"I thought you were to give me a few handy jobs today", replied Dave.

"All you have to do is secure the back door and the ground floor windows and fit a new lock to the hall door when the Sheriff is finished", stated Boylan. "Bring a nail bar in case the house is locked up".

"Where is this eviction anyway?", asked Dave.

"In Finglas, so give yourself plenty of time", replied Boylan. "I don't want the Sheriff complaining that he was kept waiting".

"Anything else?", said Dave.

"Yes, if you manage to get the keys with the old lock it can be used somewhere else", was Boylan's reply.

He turned away from the hatch and made for the Stores, handing the requisitions to the Storekeeper, who duly obliged with the materials requested, a pair of pillar hinges and a cylinder lock. One of the jobs was a new window sash, to be delivered by truck, small items and hinges, locks you brought with you. The delivery of materials depending on the location was sometimes delayed by taking small items you could at least get some work completed while deliveries were being made.

The delivery of large items such as WC., pans, wash hand basins or doors, etc. were made on the day. It had been found unsafe to deliver such items the previous day, some tenants had been known to deny any knowledge of having received them.

The first job was in St. Brigid's Gardens, a flat complex that had the reputation of being a tough place, to be avoided where possible. He had never received anything only respect from the residents. Turning into Mayor Street just as a slow, heavily laden coal truck came rolling over the cobbled stoned road. From the gates of the flats a gang of young kids charged out and with the precision of commandos in battle, born out of experience and necessity clambered up the back of the truck, like flies around a shit.

With great skill and dexterity they commenced throwing coal off the slow moving lorry. Meanwhile à second contingent appeared carrying empty sacks, which they began to fill with coal. When each sack became too heavy to carry it was quickly moved to the safety of the flats, secure in the knowledge that once inside the gates it was unredeemable.

The lorry driver, being a wise and sensible man, kept his head down, only too well aware of what was going on, or in this case, what was coming off, it was not his problem. By the end of the street, whatever coal had been taken into protective custody and distributed, affording at least some comfort from the rigors of the forthcoming Winter. The gang regrouped and prepared for the next consignment of 'cheap' coal.

With the gang on stand-by he made his way unnoticed through the entrance gates and secured the bike to the railings. Searching out the number he located it on the top balcony. Up the concrete stairs, fresh with the smell of disinfectant from the early morning 'wash-down', onto the balcony. Setting down the box of tools he paused to watch the antics of the gang below as they lined up to attach the next lorry that had just turned the corner.

Set amid the many clotheslines that littered the yard below were the coal sheds, open and ready to receive the ill-gotten spoils. Knocking on the flat door it was opened by a half-dressed boy who enquired, "what do you want Mister". "I'm from the Corporation" he replied.

"It's a man from the 'Corporation', from the well of the flat a voice cried out. "What in the name of God are you doing here?".

"I've to fit a pair of hinges to the toilet seat", he called back.

"Come back in an hour or so, I'm trying to get the children off to school".

"See you later", he replied, gathering his tools and heading for the Caretakers' dugout", where he was assured of a warm welcome.

Martin the Caretaker was a well built, grey haired man with a magnificent pair of eyebrows that dominated his lively, round face. A former Captain of the great Dublin team of the 20s and 30s, much respected for his kindness, even hard men that bowed to no one greeted him as a friend. Having spent many years working in America before returning to his present basic position as a Caretaker, being the kind of man he was he never for one moment resented his position in life.

The 'dug-out' was a small meter-room buried beneath a concrete stairs that served as both a lock-up and a meeting place for many of the maintenance staff who happened to be working in the area. With no facilities provided for the preparation of meals each was left to make whatever arrangement they could. Over a cup of tea the affairs of the day were discussed and debated.

That particular morning the debate centred on the famous long count in the Dempsey-Tunney fight. Joe Gargan, the Plumber who, in his younger days, had done some boxing, his flat nose was evidence of his participation, maintained that Tunney had beaten the count. This was disputed by an old Bricklayer named Tim Noonan who declared, "I should know, I was at the fight".

This took everyone by surprise, especially Joe who considered himself better informed than most, on account of his own experience in the ring.

"I bow to your superior knowledge", said Joe. "I didn't know you worked in the States".

"What part of America?", enquired Martin, interested to hear.

"I wasn't in America", said a straight-faced Tim.

"But you said you were at the fight", cried Joe.

"I was, in the Cinema", came the reply.

The debate collapsed into laughter.

"For God's sake, Martin, let me out of here", said Joe, furious at being had, and it was indeed time to go.

Returning to the flat he found the door standing open, knocking, to be greeted by a far off voice.

"If that's the Corpo man, come in".

"Yes Missus", he answered quietly.

"Don't just stand there", she replied loudly, "come in".

He entered the living room to find the woman of the house sitting at a table in the centre of a large dark room. A smouldering cigarette balanced on the edge of a crowded ashtray that had not been emptied in days. The table was laden down with the remains of a hurried breakfast, mugs, glasses, a half-empty milk bottle, a bowl of unfinished porridge. He glanced at the face behind the smoke screen, a face that had hard times written all over it, the eyes displayed a sadness, bordering on despair.

"Would you like a cup of tea, Mister?", she asked in a deep voice.

"No thanks Missus", he replied, "just had a cup with the Caretaker".

"You sure", she insisted, reaching to clear a corner of the table.

"Stay where you are Missus", he said, dreading the thought of more tea. "I won't be long".

"Fire away", she laughed, "the toilet is all yours".

He turned into the narrow toilet and was struck by an overpowering smell, his first move was to flush out the filthy pan. The old hinge bolts were buried in rust, the only safe way to remove them from the pan was with a hacksaw. Taking a deep breath he knelt down over the open pan to reach the bolts underneath and commenced cutting the heads off the bolts.

Great care had to be exercised. One hasty move, one careless thrust and the pan would break, all the time coming up for a lung full of air. To break a pan would be a disaster and would not endear you to the Foreman, apart from the replacement pan, a Plumber had to be found plus a special order signed by the Inspector. Sometimes it was impossible to get a matching pan, which in turn meant a new cistern as well.

Between bouts of heavy breathing and cutting with the hacksaw he slowly removed the bolts, he lost no time in completing the job. Not bothering to even wash his hands he said, 'Good morning' to the woman of the house who remained seated at the table and retired to the Caretaker's wash-room to scrub up with plenty of 'Carbolic' soap.

With relief he peddled over the bridge leading to East Wall and quickly located the house on Bargy Road. The door was opened by a solid looking woman enveloped in a floral apron, as was the fashion.

"What can I do for you Son?", she asked firmly.

"Corporation, Missus", he replied! "I've to fit a new window for you".

On hearing this her face softened slightly, "Come in please", she said pulling open the hall door. "It's about time too, do you know how long I had to wait, three months".

"I only got the docket this morning, Missus", he answered quietly, well accustomed to remarks like that, "and it takes time to make something like a new window sash".

"But, three months, I ask you", she replied. "anyway, better late than never".

Securing his bike to the railings he followed the woman through the narrow hallway into an equally narrow kitchen. beneath the window, the remains of breakfast filled the sink. Beside it a gas cooker obscured one half of the window, naturally the side with the defective sash. Bubbling away on the cooker was a large cast-iron pot, the contents of which defied description. Was it a stew, a coddle, perhaps even pigs feet. A layer of multi-coloured grease, beneath which rumbled some mysterious and potent substance, that any self-respecting 'Witch Doctor' would have been proud of.

"Would you like a cup of soup, Son?", the woman enquired, "warm you up".

"No thanks, Missus", he replied hastily, "never take anything between meals".

"It's no trouble, Son", she said, reaching for a cup. Not wishing to hurt her feelings but at the same time concerned for his own wellbeing, he suggested.

"Perhaps you could move the pot off the cooker so then I can get at the window".

The woman carefully lifted the boiling pot on to the draining board leaving him to remove the back off the cooker. The defective sash had a coat of grease and dust accumulated over the years. He scraped the heavy coating from the sash and taking great care not to break the glass, he levered the sash out.

Taking the new sash that had been delivered that morning outside he trimmed the joggles and began fitting the sash, a straightforward operation. With the new sash in place he returned to the kitchen and fitted the casement window stay. The work complete he set about removing the glass from the defective sash to assist the glazier. Most of the glaziers welcomed this assistance, a Carpenter is better equipped to take a sash apart. Some of the older glaziers would take exception claiming it was their job and threatening to call the Union as he knew Gerry the glazier well, he was not concerned.

Just then a loud knock on the door heralded the arrival of the said Gerry, as usual whistling cheerfully, be breezed into the kitchen wishing all present a very good morning. A real happy-go-lucky medium-sized young man with premature grey hair, making him appear older than his years, his rosy-red cheeks in contrast to his grey hair.

"Would you like a cup of soup, Son?", enquired the woman of the house, determined to inflict her magic potion on someone. Before Dave could give him the nod, Gerry replied with his customary enthusiasm.

"Certainly, Missus", not realising he had probably signed his own death warrant.

The kind woman reached into the steaming pot and produced a cup of the 'magic' brew. Gerry took one look at its contents and pretended to take a mouthful.

"God, that's great soup, Missus", said Gerry cheerfully, trying to conceal his true feelings. The woman thanked him and left the room. One second later Gerry threw the contents out the open window, relieved.

With the glass removed he had the sash glazed in no time. All that remained was to trim the surplus putty from inside the window as the last sliver of putty fell away the woman returned to the kitchen.

"What about another cup of soup", she asked firmly.

"No thanks Missus", replied an appalled Gerry.

"I insist. There get that into you Son", answered the kind-hearted woman, handing him a large steaming mug of soup.

He was trapped, no escape this time, the woman stood between him and the door watching as he forced himself, against his better judgement to swallow the 'Soup'. His face turned the colour of his premature grey hair, in anticipation of having his stomach pumped later that day, vowing never to partake of any food or drink offered. He reported sick for the rest of the week.

He headed back to Martin's place for lunch, to find a card game in progress, between Joe the Plumber, his mate and Martin with another Caretaker named John. He sat having his lunch and observed it always amazed him how they could remember to the last card what had been played.

The name of the game was 'Dawn', the skill displayed remarkable, with little conversation as they concentrated on the cards played. Sometimes there would be an odd post-mortem at the end of a long game, more times than not it was silent card playing.

At 1.30 sharp the game finished. There was always the possibility of a raid by the Foreman or the Timekeeper, in spite of the fact that no canteen facilities were provided for the staff .

It is a good spin to Finglas with a box of tools on a bike, up the N.C.R. by Belvedere Place, over Binn's Bridge and on to the Whitworth Road. No matter how many times you travelled Whitworth Road it was always a long hungry road with the wind in your stomach. Passing Drumcondra Hospital he waved to the open-air patients stretched out in beds with only a glass roof to protect them from elements. It was something he could never understand, especially in the depths of Winter, how such an apparent harsh treatment could provide a cure for TB then what did he know about it anyway.

Arriving at the appointed place with time to spare a knot of people, mostly women, had gathered outside the house, arms folded in anticipation of the Sheriff's imminent arrival. He decided to wait down the street till the Sheriff showed with his staff, he found the whole affair distasteful. Shortly afterwards the Sheriff's car pulled in and the Bailiffs lost no time in removing the pitiful remains of a lost home.

The lady of the house stood on the footpath her arms wrapped around two small children, in a state of shock, her face displayed utter confusion. Making himself as inconspicuous as possible he slipped in the open door and secured the house before fitting the new lock to the hall door. he could feel the anger of the people outside, an anger that manifest itself with remarks about the Corporation evicting people in this day and age.

For himself he agreed but there was nothing he could do. Surely there must be a more humane and sensitive method of dealing with a situation like this. He resolved to inform the Foreman that next time to get someone else to do their dirty work.

With the ceremonial locking of the door the lady of the house broke down and sobbed bitter tears, which in turn affected the children, who, on seeing their Mother break down, screamed uncontrollably. This raised the level of emotion for those present who had come to offer support to the victim. Abuse was hurled at all those associated with the eviction causing Dave much grief.

He heard that the husband had travelled to England in search of work, some time before, after initial period of sending money home it had stopped, leaving the woman to rear two small boys on her own. It brought home to him how strong his mother had been and how difficult it had been for his father, getting home once or twice a year, during those dangerous War years, things haven't changed much.

Making himself scarce he made tracks for the Depot. Today was pay-day, wouldn't do to be late for that. The pay car arrived at 4 o'clock and for an hour before men began making their way in the direction of the Depot. They could be observed moving slowly in the many side streets. They kept to the side streets for fear of incurring the wrath of the Foreman or the timekeeper for leaving their post too soon.

The nearer one got to the Depot the larger the numbers grew, a steady stream became a torrent that burst on to the street with the arrival of the 'blessed' pay car. As your name was called you stepped forward and collected your pay packet, with much good natured banter from the happy crowd, remarks like, "See the robber passing by", or "You have a nerve putting out your hand for money" and "Hey, ate the work", rang out. For most, it was straight to the nearest 'Bookies' or the Pub.

At the entrance to the narrow street could be seen wives and their children waiting for a husband to get paid, a few men knowing this slipped out a back entrance through the Cleansing Depot at the rear to avoid giving their families money. It was insulting to their families, practically begging in the public street in an effort to sustain the family. Most of the crew had no respect for such 'lousers' and told them so in no uncertain terms. It had been a long ordinary day.

The Joiner Shop.
Andy Kinsella, Jim Farrington, Vincent Flood.

The Joiner Shop

He turned the corner off the Coombe into the short Ardee Street. The air was filled with the terrible, obnoxious smell emanating from O'Keeffes, the knackers.

"God, what a stink", he said to himself, "why do the people put up with such a nuisance right in the heart of the city?".

After bouncing over the uneven cobbled stones he rounded the turn into Cork Street. Dismounting from his bike he walked slowly into the open yard of the Joiner shop, not knowing what to expect.

It was drab; the grey unplastered blockwork gave the place an unfinished look, piles of new doors and sashes stacked 6' high were scattered about the untidy yard. Placing the bike against the wall he strolled through a passageway of sashes to what appeared to be an office. he opened the door and walked in; his ears were assailed by the noise of machines all going full blast; he stood and surveyed the scene.

At each machine men with heads down beavering away producing the many components of joinery. On the right hand side the white aproned joiners were in the process of assembling mostly sashes, surrounded by neat piles of finished sashes.

"Can I help you?", said a sharp voice, over the noisy machines. Turning he was confronted by a medium sized man in a plain brown suit. The look on his face was enough to turn milk sour. he took an instant dislike to him. The hard-lined face with fierce brown eyes that matched his brown suit appeared to be looking through him like x-ray eyes.

"I was told to report here", he replied in his normal voice.

"What did you say. I can't hear above the sound of the machines", came the barked reply.

"I'm to report here for work", he shouted back.

The expression on yer mans face softened slightly, then reset itself. "Come into the office please, he answered loudly, turning quickly and gesturing for him to follow. he led the way to what can only be described as a glorified sentry box, masquerading as an office.

Up a short flight of steps, its raised position gave a perfect view of the workshop and, more important, the workers.

"My name is Tim, I'm the Foreman-in-Charge here", he said after closing the door. "As you can see we run a tight shop here".

"I can see that", he replied. "By the way, my name is Dave".

"Welcome aboard, as they say in nautical circles. I presume you have experience of working in a Joinery shop", enquired the Foreman.

"Yes, served my time in one", answered Dave, trying to assess the situation.

"What about woodworking machines?", asked the Foreman.

"Not too keen on them, it's a few years since I last used them, prefer to work a bench", he replied trying not to be awkward at the same time, making known his preference.

"For the moment we have sufficient bench-hands", said the Foreman, "you can start on a simple machine".

Dave detected a hint of put-down in his voice, but he let it pass for the moment.

"Leave your tools in the office, you won't need them for the moment", said the Foreman.

What about my bike, it's outside?", asked Dave.

"You can put it in the workshop for now, there is a secure shed in the yard", he answered, "follow me".

He went down the steps two at a time heading straight up the shop with Dave in pursuit. A few heads turned as he passed, all the faces were strangers to him. The planing machine was almost completely obscured behind pallets laden down with rough timber waiting to be machined.

"We have to clear this lot out of the way to make room for more of the same", shouted the Foreman, who reached down and switched on the machine, that roared to life, adding to the already high level of noise.

"Have you ever worked a planing machine like this before?", called the Foreman who then proceeded to demonstrate, "you do a face side and edge on the surface planer, then underneath for thickness".

Dave nodded in agreement, no point in trying to speak over the noise.

"I'll leave you to it, see how you get on", shouted the Foreman and with that he was off down the shop, chin out, eyes straight ahead, like a pointer dog on a shooting trip.

Dave began the process of planing the timber; first he took a length of rough timber and, holding it firmly it was passed over the open blades of the machine, a layer of timber was removed leaving the timber smooth. It was then retrieved and placing the finished side against the right angle fence it was passed over the blades again. The finished timber was stacked on an empty pallet and the whole process repeated.

Forward two steps, back two steps, repeat, two steps forward, two steps back, over and over again, so many times that it became a dull, dreary, monotonous chore. All the time the open razor-sharp mouth of the machine stared out, one lapse of concentration and you were minus a finger, a hand or worse.

The very thought sent shivers through him, having witnessed just such an accident years before when a fellow apprentice lost the tops of his fingers on a similar machine. Having been given the gruesome task of cleaning up after the accident the shocked face of the boy and the blood-splattered machine was etched in his mind forever.

The more he thought of it the more isolated he felt, not a soul he knew in sight, just an occasional glimpse of the Foreman strutting about the place trying to look important. None of the other staff even looked in his direction, they were too busy with their own work.

Time dragged on endlessly; 11 o'clock, midday and still he continued with his aimless tasks, forward and back, slow, slow, quick, quick, slow, like some mechanical figure on a music box. Having completed the last piece of timber on the surface planer the next stage was to run each length of timber underneath, through the thicknesser.

The only difference was he had to walk around the machine to remove each length of timber and place it on an empty pallet. It was back to the same again and again, mind sapping work, not as dangerous as the surface planer but just as repetitive. To break the monotony he would count the number of steps taken for each operation, he would try putting four pieces at a time through the machine but it changed nothing. In with the timber, walk around the machine, remove the timber, return and in it went, each length had to be put through the machine twice.

Watching the clock as it approached 1 o'clock he wondered no one made a move, so he switched off his machine, relieved.

"What may I ask are you doing?", came the sharp voice of the foreman.

"It's 1 o'clock, lunch-time", Dave answered.

"Still two minutes to go", replied the Foreman as he switched on the machine, "you only stop when I blow the whistle".

Dave looked at him thinking he was hearing things.

"You must be joking", said Dave loudly, wondering was he being affected by the noise and the monotony, this was unreal.

"I never make jokes", answered the Foreman sharply.

"I can see that", replied Dave quietly.

"What did you say?", said the straight-faced Foreman.

"Nothing", answered Dave, still finding it hard to credit that this was not some mad nightmare, restarting the machine with two minutes to 1 o'clock; he can't be serious, what had he landed himself in.

The whistle sounded and immediately the machines began to wind down. Dave followed suit, his ears responded to the reduced noise level, the quietness affected his balance for a minute or two.

Men rushed from the shop, no doubt heading for the canteen, an oasis of peace and tranquillity, and hot drinks. He followed at a leisurely pace, his ears adjusting to the silence. Reaching the bright coloured canteen it was crowded with men drinking mugs of tea and sandwiches and plenty of chat. No heads were raised in welcome, a strange muted crowd indeed, no one making a gesture of welcome. He had his lunch and buried his face in the morning paper. To blazes with them he thought to himself, "the onus was on them to offer the hand of friendship".

One thing missing was a game of cards; he had never been on a job where some sort of card game was not in progress, it was a way of life.

At precisely 1.30 the door burst open and the stern-faced Foreman marched in, whistle at the ready; it was the signal to return to work. Some of them were out the door before the whistle even sounded. Dave was the last to vacate the Canteen, no doubt noted by the Foreman who gave him a long hard look.

By the time he reached the machine the place was awash with noise, each machine adding a few more decibels to the already high level of noise. More of the same; his feet were beginning to feel the strain of standing in the same place for hours and hours on end. He was soon covered with a layer of fine dust, it was everywhere, up his nose, in his hair and even his eyebrows were covered white.

Slowly the hands of the clock crept laboriously on, the necessity to concentrate when working the surface machine began to diminish, forcing him to stop and shake himself from time to time. It was bad enough being stuck here, the last thing he needed was to do something stupid. Around 4 o'clock he switched off the machine and went to the toilet, more a release from the place than anything else.

Just to sit on a WC pan, away from the noise and dust might not appeal to everyone, but to him it was heaven. Closing his tired eyes he sat back, feet resting against on the door he relaxed, letting this nightmare fade away, only to be abruptly awakened from his reverie by loud hammering on the door.

"Are you near finished in there", cried out a voice, "if I have to wait any longer I'll shit in my trousers".

"No rest for the wicked", he murmured to himself, before opening the door to a small middle-aged man, his face red with anxiety.

"Thanks, I just made it", he said.

"What's wrong with the other toilet?", asked Dave.

"That's only for the Foreman", replied the man.

"You mean to say, there is only one toilet for about twenty-five men and yer man has one to himself", said a disbelieving Dave.

"I'm afraid so, sorry, no time to talk but ......". The door slammed shut.

Back at the machine he worked away, down to the last piece of timber. Now at last he might get a break from the blasted machine. Looking around for yer man, not a sign, maybe he had dropped dead, no such luck, the devil looks after his own. Behind him a large pair of sliding doors burst open like a set of lace curtains, through which a four-wheeled bogey appeared with a forest of timber ready for machining.

It seemed to have a life of its own as it moved from side to side like a drunken 'Dalek' in his direction. Stopping right beside him the bogey was withdrawn, leaving him to stare at more of the same. Not a word was uttered by the man in the cap pushing the bogey, just a nod of the head, before he retired behind the sliding doors.

Was he now destined to spend the rest of his life on this bloody machine; how unlucky can you get. Suddenly it fell silent, all machines ceased, a power failure perhaps, the men left their machines and began brushing their clothes. Glancing at his watch it was five minutes to five.

They gathered beneath the clock, chatting between themselves. He quickly joined them, all eyes were fixed on the clock, as they waited patiently for the second hand to plumb itself. The whistle sounded. From the way the Foreman blew the whistle it sounded more like a retreat to him; the long, long day was over.

Nothing was further from his mind when he had left for work that morning, like any other Monday morning, arriving at the Maintenance Depot with plenty of time to spare. As always the Depot was crowded with the usual good-natured gang. Much attention was given to any latecomers who came running in an attempt to beat the clock.

He made his way through the crowded passageway with the blank wall of the stores on one side and the glass windows of the Foreman's office on the other. Behind the glass the Foremen were preparing to issue the work to each tradesman, in the form of Works Orders, that detailed the work that was to be carried out.

The opening of the hatches heralded the beginning of another week on the 'Zone', as this type was called. Names were called and each, in their turn, presented themselves to give account of the previous day's work and receive new Works Orders.

"Dave, you are next for shaving", said one of his mates. "Boylan looks to be in a foul mood this morning".

"What's new?", he replied.

Moving to the hatch he presented himself.

"That's a fine morning, Paddy", he said cheerfully. He had a good working relationship with Paddy Boylan.

"We'll see about that", said Paddy in a gruff voice. "Have you your tools with you?".

"Certainly, I always have", Dave answered, a strange request indeed.

"Well, get your tools and a white apron together, you are to report to the Joiner Shop, as of now".

"You mean, right away", replied Dave with astonishment.

"Do you want me to write it down for you?".

"But why me!".

"Your name came out of the hat, so get on your bike and best of luck".

"I'll need it, thanks for nothing", said Dave. Turning away from the hatch he crossed to where his mates were standing.

"You look like you have seen a ghost, what's up?", enquired one of them.

"I'm shifted to the Joiner Shop in Cork Street".

"Holy Jaysus, did you have a row with Boylan?".

"No, can't understand it myself".

"He must have seen you sneaking off early some evening".

"I heard that's an awful kip of a place, yer man in charge is an animal, you nearly have to get permission to go to the toilet".

"What are you going to do. If I was you I'd go sick, they would have to send someone else in your place".

"Anyone like to volunteer to take my place", Dave asked, more in hope than anything else.

This suggestion was greeted with silence, sympathy they had for Dave's predicament, but he was asking too much.

Having said goodbye to his mates, whose friendship he had enjoyed, he headed off to an uncertain future. Was it as bad as reported. People tend to paint a dark picture in the hope, no doubt, that one goes prepared for the worst that never really materialises.

He didn't know it them but he was never to see anyone of that 'crazy gang' again.

Next morning it was with a certain amount of trepidation he arrived in the yard, the overhanging awful smell of O'Keeffes was everywhere. Expecting to find the staff gathered chatting, as in other section, he was greeted by an empty yard, not a soul in sight.

Mystified, he ventured into the workshop, to discover the staff standing by their places of work, waiting for the whistle to sound, a far cry from the previous section. Checking his watch to ensure he was on time he made his way towards the blessed machine. Before reaching it the whistle rang out and immediately the place became alive. Machines roared to life, shattering the silence. The bench-hands commenced work and the Foreman was up like a shot to quickly inform him that they began at 8.30 sharp. It was back to the same routing as yesterday, that same continuous, weary, boring, thankless work.

The days dragged by, no change. The days became weeks, then months, at which stage he was beginning to consider giving up the job.

Once or twice he approached the Foreman, requesting a change to a bench, but his request was dismissed out of hand, almost with disdain as though he had a nerve to question the Foreman's judgement.

What he missed most of all was contact with people, especially the tenants, they were great. No matter how poor their circumstances you were always made welcome. Never once was he treated with less than courtesy, even in the supposedly notorious flat complexes, the little you did in the way of repairs was appreciated.

Slowly he began to make contact with the staff; well some of them having only ten minutes tea-break and a half-hour lunch, left little time for conversation. He was intrigued by their passiveness, they appeared to be scared stiff of the Foreman, who used his authority to intimidate them. His own relationship with the Foreman was nil, he was perceived as being an outsider and a possible troublemaker.

Unhappy as he was he kept his thoughts to himself in the hope of a reprieve, but none was forthcoming. An incident one afternoon, when his concentration lapsed, a short length of timber he was working on the surface planer shot from his hand and struck the wall behind him, finally made him decide to do something. That evening he left early, filling in the necessary form that cost him an hour's pay, he went to see the Union.

The following morning, armed with the advice from the Union, instead of going to the machine he placed himself at a bench, white apron and all. His action was closely observed by the others, keen to see what the Foreman's reaction would be. They did not have long to wait. The Foreman came storming down the shop, the look on his face would have stopped a runaway train. Bracing himself for what was to come.

"What, may I enquire, are you doing here?", said the Foreman, his dark eyes blazing with anger. "I decide what you do here".

"I have been advised by my Union that a Tradesman has the option of working a machine or not", he stated firmly, keeping his voice steady in the face of the Foreman's intimidation. "I am exercising that option".

"This is a very serious matter, I would advise you to return to the machine before it is too late", said the Foreman forcibly.

It was obvious his authority had never been called into question before.

"I repeat, I will not work any machine again, for you or anyone else", replied Dave. It was now or never. If he weakened now he was destined to spend the rest of his days handcuffed to the blessed machine. The thought strengthened his resolve.

"You do realise the consequences of your action", answered the Foreman, sharply, fearing loss of face might undermine the authority he had built up over the years. "Return to the machine and I will endeavour to overlook this transgression".

"Sorry, no can do, I'm a tradesman. That work is for wood-machinists", he said calmly, his nerve was holding, but only just.

"Unless you follow my instructions immediately I will be forced to notify the Inspector. After that it is out of my hands".

Dave just shook his head, half afraid to speak in case his voice revealed his true state of mind.

"You leave me with no alternative", he stated and with that he made straight for the telephone to inform the Inspector.

Dave opened his toolbox and went through the motions of sharpening a chisel, more for something to do, as he awaited the Foreman's return. He could feel the eyes of the others on him, perhaps they thought he was striking a blow for them, he didn't feel like a hero, more a victim.

Being a single man with no ties, a born pacifist, confrontation was not his style, he tended to roll along avoiding trouble, quite happy to work away and not get too involved in the affairs of the day. He had his football at weekends to look forward to, always feeling safer in a crowd, now he was being forced to make a stand to preserve his sanity.

The Foreman appeared like magic beside the bench, the expression on his face only added to Dave's fears; was this the end of the road, it was not too late to turn back. The yellow feathers of a chicken flashed across his mind; if he failed now he had only himself to blame.

"Take your tools and follow me", he snapped. Out into the yard and up an outside staircase to a large loft, littered with broken ladders. Double ladders, push-up ladders, 40-0 and 60-0 telescope ladders, all in need of repairs.

"You want to work on a bench, now is your chance", he said with a thin smile. "New rungs, fittings, screws, all you need, take your pick".

Alone in the quietness of the loft he didn't know whether to laugh or cry, peace he had in abundance but he was still on his own.

Relieved to be away from the noisy machines he soon adjusted to the solitude imposed on him. At least it presented him with an opportunity to use his skills, albeit, a different kind of skill. Making joinery does not compare with repairs to ladders. In many ways the repairs are more important. Safety is of the essence, it means checking for defects and peoples' lives will depend on the finished product.

During the course of the day the Foreman would burst in the door in the hope of catching him idle, without as much as a word one way or the other. In effect he had been sent to 'Coventry'.

Free from the Foreman's oppressive presence he soon settled down to a routine, taking each type of ladder in its turn, leaving the long ladders to last. It appeared to annoy the Foreman that someone was capable of working without constant supervision. It exposed his insecurity, reflected his lack of trust in other people. Over the next few weeks he ploughed his way through the repairs, his contact with the others was minimal, confined to tea and lunch breaks.

With the pile of ladders diminishing he began to ponder 'what next', no point in asking the Foreman, who remained as tight-lipped as ever. He dismissed all thoughts of a reprieve. Came the faithful day the last ladder was finished he waited in suspended anticipation, refusing to contemplate his future.

"That's the last of them", he announced to yet another swift visit by the Foreman. No word of reply, just the usual dismissive nod of the head.

"Report to my office right away", he replied, leaving as fast as he came. It was with mixed feelings he made his way down the stairs to the every noisy shop. He could see the Foreman on the telephone. Dare he even think, ah … forget it. Knowing his luck there was probably a lorry load or more ladders on the way.

The Foreman put down the telephone firmly and left the office, his expressionless face yielding nothing. He was wracked with doubts, had he made it, or was it back to more of the same Bracing himself, fearing the worst, if he didn't get out now he would jack up the job.

"You are to report to Ballyfermot Depot tomorrow morning", said the Foreman and with no further ado he walked away, leaving a visibly shaken Dave to his own devices. Ballyfermot was ten miles from his home. So what, he had made it, he was free.

Housing Maintenance Section.
Inter-Departmental Winners 1959.

The Bockety Man

I t was one of those 'left-over' half days after Christmas, when everyone was off, except them. Naturally it was raining, that fine soft drizzle that clung to your clothes, forming like cotton wool on the folds of their heavy overcoats. The ancient and much used 'Hut' that served as both a workshop and canteen, stood in the centre of the green surrounded by a circle of quiet houses. A few coloured lights flashed intermittently, lifting some of the grey feelings that hung in the air.

A steady stream of men made their way to the shelter of the Hut, attired in various forms of waterproof clothes. Those on bicycles placed their bikes outside, securing them with the necessary lock and chain. Rainproof gear was given a good shake to remove any surplus water before being hung on a nail to drain off.

A rather subdued group of carpenters, numbering about fifteen, their spirits dampened by the weather and the necessity of having to work. None could afford the loss of even a half-day's pay. Inside the Hut the level of noise increased with each new arrival, the talk was mostly centred on them having to be at work, when the whole city was safely at home in bed.

One of the first to put in an appearance was one 'Canada Dry'. A most unusual name to say the least it was bestowed on a carpenter although some doubts were expressed as to his qualifications. He had a Union card so that was that. A large, fair haired bluffer of a man, with an accent difficult to place, he had been born in Dublin and reared in England, like many of his generation, often referred to as a half-baked Englishman.

He had worked for a number of years in Canada before returning to Dublin. It was while working in Canada that, following an unspecified illness, he was hospitalised. On release he was issued with a certificate declaring that the holder was sane. Many's the time, during heated discussions at lunch hour, he would produce the famous cert and declaring to one and all that "Have any of you got a cert to say you are not mad?" The response was quick and immediate, along the lines of, "That was Canada, it's not valid here", or "you must be mad to come back to this kip".

"Such a miserable shower", said Ned, an elderly and well respected man", "making us come in for a lousy half-day. I'm not exactly looking forward to knocking on doors this morning, you can imagine the reception we'll get".

"And they are right too", interjected 'Chippie', a small thin-faced Carpenter, "for all the work they'll get done".

"I heard that", replied the Foreman, who had been listening to the debate. "It's just another working day as far as your are concerned".

"Is that so", answered 'Chippie', "well you better go and knock on doors, you can take the abuse".

"No better man", snapped the Foreman. "If you think you are going to have a handy half-day, you have another think coming".

"Why can't we have a day out of our holidays?", asked Ned.

"I'll tell you why", said 'Chippie', "because the office staff don't like to be disturbed, records would have to be kept, it's far easier if everyone takes their two weeks in August".

"That's telling them Chippie", said Dave with a smile. He had a soft spot for 'Chippie'.

A small, thin, sallow-faced man, the inevitable cigarette stuck in his mouth, he could speak 'a mile a minute', without moving his lips. The only word he articulated properly and constantly used to express himself was the 'F' word. The only one in the crew to own a car, it was not much of a car, but a car nonetheless. Having clicked with a 'Yankee' that landed him a few hundred pounds, he invested his winnings in a run-down Mini.

At first he could be observed driving everywhere at great speed. To be offered a lift in the 'Mini' was an invitation to partake in a hair-raising escapade, once experienced never to be repeated. As the running costs began to hurt, it became a burden on his limited resources, often reduced to priming the car with a milk bottle of petrol, just to make it home.

"Anyone want a new docket?", asked the Foreman, always anxious to get things moving. Each docket represented for him a step forward to the completion of the job, in spite of the fact that at the finish of the job, he could be replaced, he being only a temporary Foreman.

A plump, round-faced Monaghan man, his rosy red cheeks like a well slapped arse, considered to be a bit of an 'eejit', used his ulcers as a means to try and gain sympathy from a sceptical and hard-boiled crew. He probably acquired the same ulcers by being out of his depth in charge of tradesmen.

How he ever got the position in the first place was a mystery to everyone, including himself.

His appearance did little to inspire respect, hob-nailed boots, a long dark blue serge suit with pants to match, the issue uniform for the general operatives, bought at a knock down price, the price of a few pints. More a nuisance than a Foreman, spending the day persecuting the crew, going from house to house as often as ten times a day. Annoying the workforce, who resented his lack of trust in them.

That the crew were mostly Dublin men and he a 'Culchie', did not help.

With the sounding of the whistle, followed by the mandatory roll call, it was time to get moving. Ned and Dave, who worked as mates, examined the new docket carefully.

"A few sashes and a new back door", said Ned. "Handy enough, we'll do the few sashes this morning, leave the door till Monday".

"You're right, the glazier won't thank us for keeping him to the last minute", replied Dave. "It being a half-day you could run into trouble".

"Too true, the few sashes will do for now", answered Ned, as they made their way in the direction of their place of work. Having worked together for the past few months they had got on like a house on fire. Dave, being the younger man, volunteered to do any of the heavy work, like hanging doors, not that Ned was incapable but out of respect for the older man.

Dave preferred to work with older men, found them much more interesting than his own age group, particularly stories about the many different jobs they had worked on. It gave him a good understanding of the history of the building trade from their side of the fence. One thing that was common to all, the building game was a hard, unrewarding, and in many ways, a cruel trade, once the shine had worn off.

Ned was a heavy set, middle-aged man, with a vast experience in all aspects of the building trade, having served for many years as a general foreman for H. & J. Martin's, one of the leaping building contractors of the day. He walked with a slight leaning to one side brought on by a hernia that he refused to have removed, preferring to leave well enough alone. His many tales of building sites and the characters he had encountered were a source of never-ending pleasure and amusement for the younger man.

Heretofore, each Carpenter had worked alone in a house doing repairs, but following an incident involving a Carpenter and a young woman the previous year, it was considered prudent to work in pairs. Which suited everyone. With two working in each house the work was completed in half the time, something that was appreciated by the tenants. In some cases, as many as twelve to fifteen sashes plus two doors were required, causing considerable disruption to a household.

In the company of others they made their way to their respective places of work, unsure of the reception they would receive. Ned and Dave, toolboxes in tow, arrived at the door. Ned immediately knocked. "Better get off the street before 'Puddin Head', starts his rounds", he said.

"He'll hardly be out chasing this today", enquired a surprised Dave.

"Are you joking, the persecution of the innocent is only in the halfpenny place", answered Ned with a laugh.

Before Dave could reply the door was opened quickly by a grey-hair woman who asked sharply.

"What do youse want, this hour of the morning?".

"Corpo, Missus", said Ned as Dave tried to make himself invisible behind Ned.

"You mean now, today", replied the startled woman.

"Yes, Ma'am, we have to replace a few windows and a new back door", announced Ned.

"But youse can't pull the place apart today", cried the woman. "For a start the family are all in bed asleep. Can't you leave it till Monday, when they are all gone back to work".

"Missus, we are not here by choice", said Ned earnestly.

"To think that only last week I went to the trouble of cleaning the windows and washing the curtains", said the woman, with a resigned expression in her voice. "Now you are going to pull out windows. Come in, will youse, I'll see what I can do".

"Thanks Missus, we'll make as little noise as possible", replied Ned.

They were ushered into the small front parlour bedecked with all the trappings of Christmas, fairy lights, holly and Christmas tree.

"Sit down for a minute till I see how things are", the woman said, taking leave of them.

"That's more like it", said a contented Ned as they made themselves comfortable in two fireside chairs. "We can observe everything through the window.

"Can't see us getting much done today", replied Dave.

"We've worked long enough. For once we might get a break", answered Ned, as he settled down to smoke a cigarette.

The door opened, giving Dave a start. Ned remained undisturbed as the woman entered the room, bearing a tray of drinks.

"Here, get some of the Christmas spirit into youse", she said with a dry smile.

"Missus, you should not have bothered", cried Ned, winking at his mate.

"I'm trying to get the drink out of the house as quick as possible, she said quietly".

She laid the tray on a small coffee table before them.

"But Missus, I don't ......".

"That's very decent of you Ma'am", interrupted Ned quickly. "Here's to your health and a happy Christmas to you and your family".

"Same to you Mister. Would you like a drop of water to go with it", asked the woman.

THE LAST CORPORATION MAN

"No thanks, Ma'am, would only spoil a good drink", answered Ned, as the woman left the room. "Ned, you know I don't drink that stuff".

"I know that, you know that, but she doesn't", answered Ned as he gently and slowly lifted the glass of malt to his lips and lowered it down the hatch.

"You mean you are going to drink two large glasses of whiskey and two bottles of stout, by yourself", said a startled Dave.

"I certainly am. The lady of the house might take umbrage if we were to refuse her generosity", replied Ned with a contented look on his well-worn face. Dave placed himself beside the window and settled down to await the 10 o'clock tea-break.

Back at the Hut, preparations were underfoot to deliver the materials required for each house. The hand-cart was being loaded by Joe, the labourer, who had got the fire going in readiness for the tea-break.

Joe was a poor, harmless sort of a character, single, living with his sister, a beak-like nose dominated his very thin face. A product of generations of poor working class, always looked as though he could use a good feed. His clothes were basic, the same clothes Winter and Summer. In cold weather a heavy overcoat, a few sizes too large for his thin frame, weighted him down almost to the point of doubling him in two.

Semi-illiterate with a natural flail for numbers, horse racing was one of his few pleasures. He was capable of making up any bet, no matter how complex, be it doubles, trebles, accumulators to the last penny and that included tax, without recourse of pencil or paper. Ask him to read a newspaper and he could hardly put two words together.

A few pints at the weekend in Carr's of High Street were his only other source of enjoyment. Mid-week, when funds were low, he would seek the assistance of Dave. Borrowing the price of the entrance fee, as he called it, with the expectation that someone would take pity on him and buy him another drink. Without fail the borrowed money was repaid immediately upon receiving his wages, his almost child-like innocence endeared him to everyone on the job.

Delivering materials, preparing the fire, making tea were his official duties; unofficially he was expected to handle all necessary bets for the crew. Another duty he performed each evening was to empty the dry toilet, a function he carried out without complaint.

A sharp knock on the door roused them from their thoughts, "Jaysus, who's that", asked Ned, nearly choking on a glass of whisky. "You are supposed to be keeping nicks".

"I'll go and see who it is. Hope it's not 'Puddin Head'", said Dave.

"If it is, don't let him in or I'm up shit creek", replied Ned as he lifted the tray of drinks out of sight.

In his haste he nearly overturned the remaining glass of whisky. To Ned the loss of a glass was far more important than any Foreman. Dave slipped out of the room, taking care to close the door behind him. Peeping out the hall door he was surprised to find another Carpenter, one Alfie Carr.

"Christ, Alfie, you put the heart crossways in me", exclaimed a relieved Dave. "We thought you were 'Puddin Head'".

"You know what thought done, pissed in the bed and thought you were sweating", laughed Alfie. "Don't compare me with that yoke, will you tell 'ate the work' it's time for hot drinks".

"More drinks", said Dave shaking his head in disbelief.

"What do you mean, more drinks", enquired Alfie, sensing something in Dave's voice. "Don't tell me that the woman of the house has been forcing Ned to indulge in some of the Christmas spirits.

"How did you, ... no, nothing like that", replied Dave quickly, "a little Christmas pudding, that's all. Hold on and we will be with you".

Turning away he informed Ned.

"All right Ned", said Dave, "it's only Alfie.

"What does he want?", enquired the bold Ned.

"He says it's hot-drinks time", replied Dave. "I better tell the woman. Missus, we'll be back in about 15 minutes, maybe by then some of the rooms will be available".

"Don't bank on it, Son", came the reply. "I'll do what I can".

"What do you mean, Alfie, sneaking up on a fella like that. Could of been caught doing anything", said a good humoured Ned, as they made their way in the direction of the Hut.

"I didn't hear much noise coming from the house, that's for sure", replied Alfie out of the side of his mouth.

"What do you mean. Why, we have the back door down ready for action", answered Ned in mock anger.

"Sure you have, I believe you, thousands wouldn't", said Alfie with a twinkle in his eye.

The grey Hut was crowded when they arrived. Spread on the table was the usual display of mugs, cups, some with handles, and others with none. Well blackened 'Billy Cans', each with its owner's trademark on it, a piece of copper wire, a twisted nail, some even had their name stamped on it. Each of them prepared their own tea, milk and was sugar added, then stirred with the Carpenter's rule. Sandwiches were the staple diet. Dave preferred coffee and got a right good slagging when he produced 'fairy cakes'.

"Easy know who is not married", cried Alfie. "'Fairy Cakes' for tea-break, enjoy it as long as you can".

"Jealously will get you nowhere", replied Dave, accustomed to such banter. "When was the last time you got 'fairy cakes'?"

"Don't pay any attention to him", interrupted Ned. "The last time he got 'fairy cakes' was when the war ended".

"Which war was that, the First War?", replied Dave with a smile.

"I'm telling you, hang on to your Mother as long as you can", said Alfie seriously. "When you get hitched you won't see many; fairy cakes'".

"We are not all as cynical as you Alfie", interjected Ned.

"You can say what you like, when a family comes along, the Father becomes a cash paying customer", responded Alfie. "You cease to exist".

"That depends on the circumstances", replied Ned.

"Don't be acting the eejit, Ned", said Alfie quickly. "You know as well as I do that you become the invisible man".

"Christ, you paint a bright picture", answered Dave, not sure if Alfie was getting it up for him.

"Officially you retire at 65 but the process begins the day you get married. You are out on grass long before that day arrives".

"If you don't get out of here quick, we'll all be out on grass", interrupted the Foreman.

"Trust you to spoil a good discussion", replied Alfie. "Where is your Christmas spirit?"

"I'll give you Christmas spirit", snapped the Foreman, not known for his sense of humour.

"That's great, I'll have a large brandy please", answered Alfie, offering his mug.

"Joe, will you clear that table so that we can get this show on the road", said the Foreman, as the reluctant crew slowly edged their way to the door.

"One other thing, I want all your timesheets, signed, sealed and on my desk before closing time, only this time I want the truth for a change".

This was greeted with a laugh from the departing crew.

"Dave, will you get a few nails and screws from the Bockety Man", asked Ned. "He'll think we are up to our eyes in it".

"If only he knew what we are really up to, he'd have a seizure", replied Dave.

The Bockety Man was an unofficial assistant to the Foreman with no standing other than being a pal of the Foreman. A small wizen-faced man, with an irritating manner, often referred to as Creepy Joe. His function was to check out all materials, sashes, doors, nails and screws, leaving the Foreman to supervise the work in progress. Treated with a certain amount of contempt by the crew, generally perceived as being a 'Lick', sometimes called a 'Squashy' Foreman (an inversion of quasi).

One of his other duties was to cut up for firewood any old doors that were returned to the Hut. Each evening the Foreman's two pannier bags were filled with this firewood and carried home to supplement his fuel supplies.

Returning to the house the lads were again admitted to the parlour by the woman who informed them that there was not a hope of getting into any of the bedrooms.

"What are we going to do?", asked a nervous Dave. "We can't just sit here till lunch-hour".

"You heard what the woman said", replied Ned seriously, "we can't disturb the family".

"But if the Foreman comes" cried Dave.

"I'll take care of him, we can make up the work on Monday", answered Ned, "when the house is empty".

The door opened and the woman appeared with another tray of drinks, which she placed on the table.

"Youse just sit there, I'll answer the door", she said and with no further ado, she left them to their own devices.

"Ah, Ned, this is too much", stated an incredulous Dave.

"I couldn't agree more", replied a wide-eyed Ned. "Shouldn't be allowed".

At the same time he reached out and before you could say 'hush to a duck', another large whiskey vanished without trace, quickly followed by a bottle of stout. The next hour witnessed the death of the tray of drinks, leaving Ned in a state.

"You know what", he muttered, his eyes displayed the effects of the free drink, "you are a lucky man".

"I'm lucky, that's a laugh coming from you" replied Dave, "how do you make that out".

"You don't drink or smoke", said a muddled Ned.

"Thank God for that", answered Dave, concerned about his mate's condition.

"That gives you a head start on everyone else", said a confused Ned.

"Just as well I don't", Dave answered. "You better stay seated or you might do yourself an injury".

"There's nothing wrong with me", replied Ned as he tried to stand up, only to fall back into the safety of the chair.

A loud knock on the door brought them down to earth, before Dave could move the hall door was opened by the woman of the house. The sharp voice of Alfie could be heard.

"Missus, have you two Carpenters working in there?", he asked.

"Who wants to know", came her curt reply.

"Just tell them it's Alfie Carr".

"Alfie Carr? Are you from Cabra, Mister", she enquired.

"Yes I am, why?", said Alfie.

"I have a cousin named Carr", she said, "used to live in North King Street"!.

"You know what, you do look kinda familiar", Alfie replied.

"I'm Peter O'Brien's daughter, Mary", came her reply.

"Jaysus, if that doesn't beat Banagher", exclaimed a surprised Alfie. "Haven't seen you since you were a little girl at your father's funeral, Lord have mercy on his soul".

"You better come and join the party, they are in the parlour", she said.

When Alfie saw the tray of empty glasses and the state of Ned he almost swallowed his false teeth with surprise. Reaching out he slowly lifted an empty glass and with sadness in his voice said. "Dead men tell no tales", lamented Alfie, "to think that the pair of you have been sitting here gulping down free drinks in a house belonging to a niece of mine, and me dying for the want of cure".

"You can count me out", replied Dave. "I never touch the stuff".

"What's wrong with you Alfie", enquired a sleepy faced Ned.

"Not as much as a spoonful left", moaned Alfie, "a fella could die for the want of a drink, might as well be in the desert".

"Will you stop complaining Alfie, you would do exactly the same given half a chance", answered Dave. "More important, will you stay with Ned while I go and get 'Chippie' to bring him home".

"Be careful, in case 'Puddin Head' finds out", warned Alfie, resigned to the fact that he was not going to get a drink.

"Be back in five minutes", said Dave, leaving the two of them to argue the rights and wrongs of the situation.

Dave was back in a few minutes with 'Chippie' in tow. With great difficulty Ned was packed into the 'Mini'. Before leaving the house he told the woman that first thing Monday morning they would be back.

When knocking off time arrived they left Ned sitting in the car outside the Hut. When the whistle sounded away they went to deliver him to his home. The 'Mini' screeched to a halt outside the house. Dave and 'Chippie', taking an arm apiece, frog-marched Ned to the door, where they propped him. Giving a few knocks on the door they returned to the car and in a cloud of smoke fumes, sped away, leaving Ned to face the wrath of his wife.

Corporation Place.
(courtesy of Jimmy Wren)

Corporation Place

"I'll get it", came the response to the ringing telephone. "It's for you Dad".

"Who is it?", he asked, fearing the worst.

"Didn't say, sounds urgent", replied his son.

"Hello, can I help you?", he enquired. "Joe, oh no, not this hour of the night", his worst fears confirmed.

"Right first time", answered the ever cheerful Joe, "and you thought you were going to see 'Match of the Day', didn't you".

"You can't be serious, it's lashing rain. You wouldn't put the dustbin out on a night like that", he replied. His heart sank at the prospect.

"Sorry mate, I've tried a few others, no joy", came the answer. "Never mind, think of all that lovely overtime you will clock up, double time after 12 o'clock".

"Never mind the sermon, just give me the details. What is it anyway?", he asked with a resigned sigh.

"Report of a leaking roof and a flooded flat", answered Joe.

"What's the address?", he asked, anxious to get going, to get finished.

No reply.

"Joe, are you still there, where is it?" he enquired, getting tired of Joe's little game.

"Wait for it - ...... Corporation Place", came the reply.

"Oh, for heaven's sake, that's above and beyond the call of duty", he answered in disbelief. "No-one is safe in that place, certainly not after midnight on a wet miserable Saturday night".

"The Dangerous Building Inspector called it in", replied Joe. "No. 61. He'll be waiting for you, away you go, the match is just about to start, wouldn't like to miss any of it, have a nice day".

He replaced the phone, looking out to see if the rain had eased off; if anything it had got worse.

"You haven't to go out in that weather, have you?", asked his wife, concerned for his wellbeing.

"I'm afraid so, I'd better ring John to come and collect me", he replied, "where's my waterproof gear, looks like one of those nights".

"You'll get your death of cold, shouldn't have answered the phone".

"It's too late now", he said as he reached for the phone. John's voice answered immediately, like he was sitting waiting for it to ring.

"John, just got a call for, of all places, Corporation Place. Will you collect Bernard on the way, I'm not going in there by myself".

"You are perfectly right, never can tell with a place like that", answered John. He could tell the note of satisfaction in John's voice. "We won't be long".

Replacing the phone he went searching for his rain gear, having become accustomed to these late night emergency calls, most of which were straightforward consisting of blocked drains, burst pipes, securing vacant houses, etc. It played havoc with his spare time, especially weekends. Should be spending more time with his family. Trying to keep a balance had to be measured against the necessity of providing for his family.

"Has Dad to go out in that weather?", asked his son.

"Unfortunately, it's part of his job", replied his wife, only too well aware of how he felt, she had similar regrets.

"It's not fair, they should get someone else, it's always Dad", answered the boy. "He never has time for anything".

"You have to understand that without the extra money we would not have much of what we take for granted", responded his wife, trying to console the boy. Whatever misgivings she might have there was no point in making it more difficult for him by complaining.

He well recalled a previous visit to Corporation Place.

The look of amusement on the face of the Foreman when he was handed a Works Order.

"There you are sundown, it's time you entered the real world", he said.

"You are not sending him there", interjected another Foreman with mock horror.

"Why not, there has to be a first time for everyone".

He stood there looking at the address. 'Corporation Place'. The very name itself was enough. He had somehow managed to avoid being sent there, it had finally caught up with him.

Stories were told, in hushed tones by hard men, men who had worked on some of the roughest building sites, yet he had seen these same men tremble at the mere mention of the name. It was going to need all his willpower and strength of character, as he headed off, no turning back. If he failed now he could never look them in the face again. Filled with fear and uncertainty he was determined to come through with his head held high.

As he drew closer the entrance loomed before him, like something out of 'Dante's Inferno'. Even the sun disappeared behind clouds, as if unwilling to shed its light on such a place. The small empty faces of hungry children, literally droves of them were everywhere, watched him with their sad eyes.

It was all he had heard and more. Five-storey buildings with railed balconies giving it a prison-like appearance. For its inhabitants it was a prison with the gates open, with nowhere to go and nothing to do, sometimes referred to as 'Sing-Sing'. His eyes searched for Flat No. 61, only to locate it on the top balcony.

Making his way up the filthy concrete stairs he was almost overcome by the combined and toxic smells of 'Jeyes Fluid' and the even stronger smell of urine, that pervaded the stairwell. It was overpowering and all embracing.

On reaching the second floor landing he came face to face with an old lady bent with age, burdened down with a heavy sack of coal. He felt obliged to offer assistance but his offer was sharply rejected.

"You want me to give you my bag of coal, do you think I'm mad or what", she retorted. "I'd never see you or the bag again", as she resumed her tortuous ascent.

Arriving at the fifth floor he stood and viewed the scene below from the safety of the railed balcony. The air was refreshing but the sight below remained grim. Little effort had been made by the local authority to try and preserve the fabric of the building, maintenance had been reduced to the minimum. It had become substandard, unfit for human habitation. The residents appeared to have given up caring.

Approaching the flat slowly, hesitating, stepping over some rubbish deposited on the balcony, he knocked on the door. No reply, he tried again. Still no reply. His heart lifted at the prospect of not being able to gain admission. He could return the Works Order saying he was unable to gain entry. Knowing the Foreman he would be told to retain the docket and try again.

The door opened abruptly and the pale face of a young girl appeared from the darkness within.

"What do you want Mister?", she enquired quickly.

"Corporation, to fix the window", he replied.

The door slammed shut and he was left to wonder what next. Uncertain what to expect he turned away, at a loss what to do, was he to go or stay.

"Come in Mister", called a voice from the now open door. He stepped forward into the gloom of the living-room, a poor looking fire was fighting for its life in the grate and losing the battle to stay alive. An equally black kettle was sitting amid the coals trying to boil. The young girl sat beside the fire blowing on the coals in a fruitless attempt to force some life into it.

The room was almost in complete darkness. Heavy curtains obscured the window, making it difficult to see anything. As his eyes adjusted to the room light he became aware of how sparsely the room was furnished with bare boards and the ever present smell of tea stewing.

"Which window do you have to fix, Mister", she asked turning to face him, her dark eyes set in the pale gaunt face of a young girl in her early teens, old before her years.

"It says on the docket, the back bedroom", he answered.

Raising herself from the chair she crossed the room and led the way into an equally dark room

A small child was standing at the end of a cot beside the bedroom door, awakened, no doubt, by the knocking on the door. The child began to cry, quietly at first, increasing the volume to a full blown howl, at the appearance of a stranger. Mercifully, the young girl lifted the child from the cot and immediately the child ceased crying.

"That's the only window here", she said, pointing to the curtained window, "must be that".

Directly beneath the window, wedged against the wall, was a double bed, obstructing access to the window. The bed was littered with a jumble of bed clothes piled high in the centre.

"Can I move the bed?", he enquired.

The prospect of having to stand on the bed to repair the sash cords did not appeal to him. He tried to shift the bed to one side but it refused to budge an inch, like it was nailed to the floor.

At that very moment the bed clothes moved, causing him to jump back.

"Missus, is there someone in the bed?" he cried.

"Ah, that's only Granny. As long as you don't step on her she won't mind", came the casual reply.

"I'll come back later, when the bed is empty", he suggested.

"Won't matter, she never gets up except to go to the toilet", she replied.

"But I can't just climb over an old woman in her own bed", he said in a shocked voice.

The young girl leaned over and whispered to the old woman.

"Granny, the man from the Corporation is going to fix the window, move over to one side so that he can get at it". A low moan emanated from beneath the bedcovers as they rolled to one side, leaving the other side clear.

He hesitated, what to do, not relishing the prospect of standing on the bed. Perhaps he could return to the Depot, tell the Foreman to get someone else. He could just see their mocking faces, hear their laughter when word got out that he had chickened out.

Holding his nerve he gingerly stepped on the bed, half expecting it to immediately collapse under the weight, his foot held firm, now the other foot. Reaching the window he drew the curtains that held out the light.

The top sash, it was always the bloody top sash. This necessitated the removal of the bottom sash to gain access to the sash weights, making the job more time consuming. With both feet firmly planted on the bed nothing moved beneath the covers. Nevertheless, he could feel something climbing up his legs, real or imaginary. Reaching down he tucked his pants in to his socks, scratching to get relief. His imagination ran riot, creating images in his mind of having to burn his clothes when he finished. The more he thought about it the more he was convinced that he was going to be eaten alive by fleas or even worse, bugs.

Conjuring up all his skills, coupled with great haste, he replaced the sash cords in record time. With a sigh of relief he stepped off the bed and beat a hasty retreat to the living room.

"That's finished, Missus", he said as he made his way to the hall door, hardly waiting to put his tools away.

"Thanks Mister", she replied, in a flat lifeless voice. The child, on seeing him, began crying again. With a quick goodbye he escaped to the safety of the balcony, pulling the door behind him, leaving the young girl to console the child.

He stood for a minute brushing real or imaginary objects from his pants, still not convinced that it was all in the mind.

He headed for the foul smelling staircase, anxious to put distance between himself and this sad place. At the next landing he encountered another young girl, hardly in her teens, trying to negotiate the slippery stairs, pulling a child laden pram behind her step by step. His offer of help was appreciated but refused. "I'm nearly there, thanks just the same Mister", she replied breathlessly. Down the last few steps and out into the open yard where he met one of the Caretakers, a large heavy set man, in full issue uniform, leaning on his brush, as is the perceived notion of all Corporation staff. He did not envy them their job, trying to keep such places in some sort of order against impossible odds, a truly lost cause.

"You must be the new man, how did you get on?" he asked, trying to read the expression on the face of the Carpenter, a simple task.

Explaining to the Caretaker the work he was obliged to undertake and the conditions he had been forced to endure. This brought a laugh from the Caretaker.

"You think that was bad, should have seen what the Plumber got this morning", he replied.

"Stop, will you, I'd rather not know. Nothing about this place surprises me".

Shortly afterwards the van arrived and away they went. Little did they realise what was in store for them.

"Bernard, hope you brought your heavy rain gear, it's a dirty night to be out".

"I sure did; wellies, southwester, the lot", came the reply. "What's the job, John mentioned Corporation Place".

"A leaking roof. Must be bad when the Dangerous Buildings called it in", he answered. "We'll soon find out".

Whenever possible he endeavoured to have Bernard along, a most intelligent and obliging man, with vast experience in all aspects of emergency work, he having worked for a number of years in the Dangerous Buildings Section. Having one you can trust and depend on made his job as a Foreman easier. Bernard's day job was Clerk/Store Man but it only served as a vehicle for his many other talents. A man of infinite patience, well regarded by his colleagues, he seemed to have telepathic powers when it came to danger. His calm presence when under pressure was reassuring to all, he always appeared to be a few jumps ahead of everyone else.

John the driver was a completely different character, a handsome looking man with a fine crop of well groomed grey hair. A permanent driver in the 'Dangerous Buildings' Section. As such he was obliged to be on call 24 hours a day including weekends. The number of hours overtime he worked was considerable. He had dedicated his life to work no matter what hour, be it day or night John answered the call. It was said of him he had cancelled his holidays on a number of occasions when overtime loomed, all in the interest of public safety of course.

Naturally he was the envy of the other drivers, who saw him as being greedy for not sharing the spoils with them.

"Jaysus, that rain is getting worse", said John as they approached the turn in Talbot Street leading to Corporation Place.

"Straight rain, goes on for ever", replied Bernard, as the wipers laboured to clear the windscreen. The van edged its way in to the open yard between the five-storey blocks of flats and stopped.

"Any sign of the Inspector?", he asked as they searched the rain-sodden night.

"He won't be far away. Once he gives the instructions he can head for home, lucky devil".

The van was illuminated by the flashing headlights of a car behind.

"That must be him, I'll go and get the details", he said jumping from the van into the pouring rain. He was back in a few minutes with the Works Order directing him to secure and make good the roof of Flat No. 57.

Leaving John with the van they climbed the dark wet staircase with the aid of a hand torch before locating the flat on the top balcony. Arriving at the entrance, he knocked at the door. A small thin-faced boy peered through the opened door.

"What do you want, Mister?", he asked.

"Is your Mammy or Daddy at home?", he enquired.

"No, Mister, they are in the pub", came the reply.

"We are from the Corporation to fix the roof".

"Come in, it's very wet in here. Some of the big fellows robbed the slates off the roof the sell in the scrap yard", he answered.

They entered the darkened flat slowly. Four children, aged between 3 and 8 were standing in the centre of the room, the only dry part.

A single candle threw its useless light in all directions, a lifeless bulb dangled from the water-logged ceiling. An infant child was standing half naked in a cot near an empty grate, the saddest, most pathetic little creature he had ever witnessed. He was shocked at the child's appearance, its dark little eyes staring at him, the eyes set in a pale face, hair hanging in curls around his shoulders.

"Is he sick?", he asked the eldest boy.

"No, he was in hospital, but he is all right now", replied the boy.

"What was wrong with him?", he enquired as he flashed the torch light around the room.

"He had 'Melongitis'" came the reply. "He only came home yesterday".

He turned to Bernard in an effort to understand the situation.

"My God, imagine sending a child to this", he cried. "Not even electric light".

"It was probably cut off. How is the hospital to know what the circumstances are", answered Bernard, just as shocked. "The best thing to do is fix the roof as quick as possible".

Telling the children to stay put, assuring them that they would return shortly, they headed for the van, only to be greeted with a hail of stones and bottles rained down upon the van from one of the balconies.

"That takes some beating, doesn't it, we leave our homes to try and help a family in distress and what do we get —— pelted out of it", cried an angry John, as he pulled the van out into the street as quick as he could.

"Drop us off at the Depot while we are getting the materials. You go and get the 'Strangler' and two other helpers", as they drove across town.

By the time they sorted out the materials the van returned with the extra staff, the materials were loaded into the van, ladders, tarpaulins, timber battens, nails, etc.

"We'll call to Store Street Garda Station on the way down, see if we can get some Gardai protection", the Foreman said.

"A good idea, we might not be so lucky this time", replied John, always concerned for the condition of the van. He took great pride in keeping it spotlessly clean inside and outside.

They pulled into Store Street behind the bus station and stopped outside the Police Station.

"Sargent, Corporation, we are trying to effect repairs to a flat in Corporation Place. We were attacked by a stone throwing gang a while ago". He asked, "any chance you could give us a little protection".

"Not a hope", replied the Sargent. "Saturday is our worst night, the only thing I can suggest is to come back about 3 or 4 in the morning when they are all asleep".

"We can't sit here waiting for them to go asleep, there is a family whose flat is open to the elements. Is there nothing else you can do", he enquired, aware of his position and the position that pertained for the unfortunate children.

"Tell you what", said the Sargent. "There is another entrance from Foley Street at the rear of the flats; you should be able to slip in without being noticed".

"Come on, we'll chance it", he said to Bernard.

"John is not going to like it", replied Bernard.

"That's too bad for him, what's the alternative", he answered. "The welfare of the children outweighs his objections".

True enough John was reluctant to go near the flats.

"I'll drop youse and the gear off and wait outside", was his response.

"You will do nothing of the sort", retorted the 'Strangler'. "How are we supposed to get out without the van".

"The van is my responsibility. If anything happens to it I'm the one who will be called to account, not you", snapped John, who appeared to be more concerned for the safety of the van than the crew.

"I'll take responsibility", replied the Foreman, as he tried to calm down things. "We will be as fast as we can".

They located the entrance in Foley Street and with the lights switched off they sneaked in and quietly unloaded the van, before hauling them up the stairs. The rain poured down with a vengeance. It was determined to make it as difficult as possible for them. Setting the ladder down on the balcony they somehow managed to drag the tarpaulin on to the roof and they set about trying to secure it.

Everyone lent a hand, fixing one side of the tarpaulin in place by using battens nailed to the existing roof rafters, not without some difficulty. In trying to fold the now soaking tarpaulin over the ridge and down the other side it was caught by the wind and, like a ship's sail, it whipped back on top of them, pinning them underneath.

They struggled to free themselves, very aware of their perilous position, clinging to the battens for dear life. After what seemed an eternity one of them crawled out the end and sitting astride the ridge began rolling back the tarpaulin, freeing those trapped beneath. And still the rain lashed them, drenching them through and through. Slowly and carefully they straddled the ridge, a leg on each side, silhouetted against the dark sky, like rain soaked chimney-pots. First one batten was nailed in place near the ridge and using that as a hand-hold they managed to secure the tarpaulin in place with the other battens.

"For God's sake, be careful", he cried as the 'Strangler' clambered down the open side of the roof. "One slip and you are a gonner".

Finally, the last nail was driven home, a relieved crew climbed down on to the balcony, exhausted. He left them to take the gear to the van, while he returned to the flat.

The same boy opened the door to his knock.

"Are your parents home yet?", he asked.

"Not yet, Mister, but the rain has stopped coming in".

Flying Shores

Dangerous Buildings

"Well, well, what have we got here?", said Billy Raymonds to the man who had just dismounted from his bike. "Dave, you are a long way from home".

"Billy, long time no see, how are things in 'Gloccamorra'", answered Dave.

"What on earth are you doing in a God forsaken place like this, this is the last outpost of civilisation", asked Billy. "Was there a falling out with Boylan or what?".

"That's the gas part of it; I'm one of the few who can get on with him", replied Dave.

"Must have dirtied your bib somewhere along the line", said Billy, "to be sent to the Dangerous Buildings, means only punishment".

"Be that as it may, I've to report to 'Cock Robin', is he about the place?", enquired Dave?

"He is down the street barricading an empty flat", replied Billy. "Don't worry, you'll hear him before you see him".

"Is he as thick as ever?", asked Dave, removing his tool-box from the bike.

"The older he gets, the worse he becomes", said Billy.,

They entered the house being used by the crew as a 'dug-out' who were in the process of demolishing decayed and vacant Georgian houses in Dominick Street. The impressive entrance, with its ornate door and fine moulded surrounds, gave way to a large spacious hall. The first thing that struck Dave was the overpowering smell, the musty, stale smell of humans and cats. Leaving his bike in the hall he followed Billy into the front drawing room, with its fine plastered ceiling, cornices and moulded architraves, that had seen better times. These former gracious homes of past opulence that were soon to be replaced by 'modern' apartments.

A fire blazed in the black hole of a grate, that had once been the focal point of the room, the once magnificent marble fire surround had long since vanished. A black galvanised bucket of water now sat on the fire in preparation for the morning tea-break.

The room was a complete mess, littered with old timber, empty cans, concrete blocks and cement bags and looked like it had not been swept in ages. The large windows were shuttered on the outside for security and to keep out the elements. The glass was, of course, missing.

"Give your 'Billy' can to Larry the nipper, he'll look after it for you", said Billy referring to the grey haired old man stoking the fire. Larry's only function was the preparation of tea, go for messages to the Works Department and more important, go to the 'bookies'. A small low sized man with rounded shoulders, his clothes were in keeping with the surroundings. Married late in life to a widow with six children, he was treated like a lodger, his unopened wage packet was taken from him each week and he was given a few bob pocket money. He supplemented his meagre income by collecting scraps of brass, copper or lead, even a few slates, which he then sold to the local scrap-merchant. If he did manage some scrap now and then nobody cared, he was considered harmless.

Billy was an entirely different character, a giant of a man, over 20 stone in weight with the strength of four men, he looked like a live version of 'Desperate Dan'. It gave him an air of authority, the unopposed leader of the crew; he would laugh at the puny efforts of others in a show of strength. One of his favourite games was with the unloading of bags of cement from a lorry, to carry one bag was enough for any man. Billy would take one bag under each arm and ramble across the yard like he was carrying two heads of cabbage. "Sit down for a minute Dave, before the gang arrives and I'll tell you a good story about 'Cock Robin', said Billy, pointing to a plank resting between two concrete blocks to form a makeshift seat. "The other day he was barricading an empty ground floor flat, not far from here".

"Is that all he ever does?", asked Dave.

"That's all he's able for. Anyway, he was nailing the timber shutters on the inside of the windows, a handy way of securing the flat".

"They are fairly big windows in those 'Georgian' houses, replied Peter, "at least 12-0 foot high".

"After much huffing and puffing he eventually succeeded in lifting one half of the shutter on to the window board".

"Did he not have a helper with him?", enquired Dave.

"You know him, thinks he can do everything on his own", answered Billy. "Holding the shutter in place with one hand, he reached for his hammer, only to discover it was not in his belt".

"Where was it?", asked Dave?

"It was lying on the floor behind him", said Billy. "He tried to reach it with his foot but it was just out of reach".

"He was on the horns of a dilemma".

"With him you never can tell, he studied his position for a few minutes trying to decide what to do", said Billy. "Should he take down the shutter, retrieve the hammer and secure the shutter or chance removing the hand supporting the shutter, make a grab for the hammer and get back before it came tumbling down".

"Don't tell me, I can guess", answered Dave.

"When we found him two hours later he was still out cold", said Billy.

"Could have been killed", replied Dave.

"He was lucky, it landed on the thickest part of him, his head", Billy said with a laugh.

"There's only one 'Cock Robin'".

"Thank God for that".

Shortly afterwards the crew arrived and a sorrier looking bunch they were, dressed in the most appalling clothes imaginable. Their hands and faces filthy dirty, the whites of their eyes shone through the blackness, like refugees from a 'Black and White Minstrel Show'. Some were in overalls, others wore old ragged and torn clothes. Those lucky enough to be permanent staff were issued each year with new overalls and boots. Others, being temporary staff, supplied their own clothes. As a result they were always poorly dressed, with ill-fitting, worn out clothes and very poor footwear.

"Dave, me oul pal, how is it going?", asked one of the crew

"Christy, don't tell me you are still getting away with it", answered Dave. "Did you not get found out yet?".

"Did you hear anything?", enquired Christy.

"Not a whisper", replied Dave.

"Have ya me knife?" said Christy.

"What knife?"

"Have ya me knife?" repeated Christy.

"Don't mind him", interrupted Billy. "He's always at that, a born messer".

"If you can't take a joke, you'd be better off dead", answered the red-haired Christy as he shook the dust from his filthy clothes, before taking his seat on the wooden bench, still smiling.

All had a ready, almost reckless sense of humour. It was surely needed, considering the type of work being undertaken at that time, the taking down of ceilings. The ceilings were of lath and plaster. You can imagine the accumulation of dirt and grime after a hundred years of occupation.

First the flooring boards were removed, leaving a catwalk around the edge. The ceilings were then punched down through each floor into the basement. With the windows also removed dust and dirt was everywhere; in their eyes, their hair and in their lungs. It was like a dirty sand storm. That all the ceilings had examples of fine Georgian plasterwork and ornate cornices mattered little to the crew, the quicker they came down the better.

Most of the crew had worked on dangerous buildings sites for a number of years. Strange as it may appear they were reluctant to transfer to some other Department where it would be financially more rewarding, easier and certainly cleaner. There was a sort of adventure to it, a battle of wits between themselves and the Foreman who, to them, represented authority. It seemed to give them a purpose, a sense of meaning to their otherwise miserable existence.

It is difficult to define their apparent reluctance to change, most of them were very sharp operators in their own way, taking no responsibility for anything except their work, feeling safe and secure in their own group.

The tea was something else, no attempt was made to wash their already dirty hands, even if they wished. There was no provision to do so. As for the toilet facilities, it does not bear mentioning. The lunches consisted of bread and jam sandwiches. The closer it got to the end of the week, more likely it would be 'Prairie' sandwiches, open spaces between each slice of bread. The 'Nipper' was given tea and sugar every morning by each man, the contents were then emptied into a large galvanised bucket of water and then boiled.

The 'communal' bucket was then placed in the centre of the floor for all to partake of. The milk was then added to the 'magic brew' giving a little colour to the dark brown tea, each in their turn took a fill from the bucket.

Jam jars, chipped mugs, cups without handles, milk bottles, and even the old hair-oil bottle were used to drink from. The drinking utensils were placed on the dirty floor and when a refill was called for it was wiped on the side of their pants, before being plunged into the waiting bucket. Dave observed this exercise with horror, grateful he had his own cup and can. The very thought of having to partake in the tea bucket appalled him.

The 'Happy Minstrels' seemed oblivious of the danger to their health. What the long term effects would be only time would tell. One particular character caught Peter's eye, known as 'Louis the Lamb', a long, skinny hungry looking man about 50, his lean frame disguised a tough hardy fellow. Renowned for his lack of fear when it cam to heights, often observed standing on the parapet wall of a dangerous building, four-storeys high, at the same time he was demolishing the very wall from beneath his feet with a sledgehammer.

He sat there on an upturned bucket, his mug of tea beside him on the dirty floor. From his pocket he produced his lunch. Peeling away layers of paper he took out a large 'pigs foot' and began munching it, washing it down with mouthfuls of tea. After a while the combination of dirt and grease merged, causing it to stream down his blackened face in a disgusting mess. In due course the sleeve of his filthy jacket was called into play to remove the surplus.

The remains of the 'pigs foot' was cast into the fire where it blazed momentarily before being consumed by the flames.

"Do you have to eat such stuff", enquired Billy, not in the least impressed with what he saw.

"I don't ask you what you had for your lunch", replied Louis sharply.

"I know, but Jaysus look at the mess", implored Billy. "It's bad enough here without having to witness that".

"We all need a certain amount of fat to keep out the cold", Louis answered.

"I'll agree with you on that, but it is supposed to be on the inside", said a disgusted Billy, "not running down your face".

"If you don't like what you see, look the other way", was the answer he got.

The loud banging of the hall door heralded the arrival of 'Cock Robin' who was acting in a temporary capacity as a charge-hand.

"What did I tell you, you'd hear him before you'd see him", said Billy as 'Cock Robin' burst in the door, nearly falling over a concrete block in the process.

"Be careful, you might knock over that concrete block", said one of the crew. The remark was ignored by 'Cock Robin'.

"Any tea left?" he asked.

"Plenty of black tea; unfortunately the milkman didn't come this morning", replied Billy.

Cock was a tall, rangy man, about 60 with matted grey hair, sadly in need of cutting, wearing a boiler-suit, a claw-hammer permanently stuck in his belt. He was 'one of the boys', having been in the old I.R.A. during the so-called 'troubles'. It was said of him that he had taken part in a mass escape of Republican prisoners from Mountjoy prison. Some were unkind enough to suggest that when escaping over the wall he had landed on his head, that had left him slightly off centre, with a strange wild look about him, not helped by the fact that he was also 'gunner-eyed'.

When speaking to him one was never sure if he was looking at you or the fella beside you. A carpenter by trade the only work he ever seemed to undertake was work related to demolition, just give him some timber, galvanised iron, plenty of 4 inch nails and he would be in his element.

"There's been a change of plans this morning", announced 'Cock'. "I want you all for a special job".

"You mean, no more ceilings", asked Billy hopefully.

"Not for the moment", replied 'Cock'. "We have to strip the roof of a house, just taken-in-charge, in case the materials go missing".

The news was greeted with a sigh of relief by the black-faced crew. Ceilings were the worst part of the job, any little respite was welcome.

"Cock, I was told to report to you", said Dave, when things settled down.

"The very man", replied 'Cock'. "I've a set of flying shores for you, just down the road. You can take Christy and George with you".

"What houses are they?", enquired Dave?

"Between 7 and 8, on the other side of the street", said 'Cock'.

The break over, Dave and his two mates made off down the street to survey the site, before commencing work on the flying-shores. The rest of the crew followed 'Cock' to a vacant house on the corner of Parnell Street up the stairs and then by ladder onto the roof.

"I want the slates removed carefully, then we can start work on the lead valley", said 'Cock' as the crew stared at the size of the lead valley, trying to estimate its worth on the open market.

They began removing the slates, saving as many as possible for future use. Each bundle of slates was carried down by hand and left in neat piles to await the arrival of the lorry. The last slate was taken away, then came the big prize, the lead valley.

"We'll never manage to get it down the stairs in one piece", commented Billy, having felt the quality of the lead, and with his experience realised its value.

"It's not going down the stairs", replies 'Cock'.

"If it's not going down the stairs", asked Billy, "how do we get it off the roof?".

"Simple really, we just cut it in short lengths, then lower it over the parapet directly onto the lorry", announced 'Cock' triumphantly. From his pocket he produced a snips. "I don't trust you lot for one minute".

"Are you suggesting that we would even think of interfering with the removal of such 'dirty old lead'", replied Billy, winking at his mates.

"You lot would rob the eye out of my head and come back for the eyelashes", answered 'Cock'.

"How could you for one moment think such a thing, it's a slur on our characters", said Billy with a mocked pained expression on his fat face.

The lead was taken up, cut into short lengths, rolled then secured with a rope and dragged to the parapet, after making sure the lorry was in place it was slowly eased over the edge.

"Two of you take hold of the rope behind me", shouted 'Cock' as he leaned back holding the rope tightly. Two of the lads grabbed the rope, as another stood on the parapet to direct operations.

Billy took one look at what was happening. All that lovely lead disappearing before his very eyes. He made a dash down the stairs to the first floor landing and over to the window. He was just in time to see a precious roll of lead passing the window and onto the lorry.

The parapet man signalled and the rope was returned and the same procedure repeated. Only this time as the roll of lead passed the window it was rescued by the strong arm of Billy who maintained the tension on the rope and with the other hand removed the lead roll. The parapet man quickly realised what was happening and again signalled the rope's return. Every second roll in its turn was taken into protective custody, mission complete. It only remained for the slates to be loaded and away the lorry went to the Stores.

What they were doing was not right but the nature of the work was such that it was impossible to estimate the salvage value. Also the work was so distasteful, dirty and dangerous, it was hard to blame them for trying to make a few bob for themselves.

When Dave and his mates returned for lunch they could detect a certain buzz in the air; something was up. No sooner had they gathered around the infamous tea-bucket when in the door charged Joe, shouting for 'Cock'.

"What's wrong with you", snapped 'Cock'. "I'm having my lunch".

"Forget the lunch, this is more important", said a breathless Joe.

"What could be more important than lunch", answered 'Cock'.

"You better come quick or you are in trouble", replied Joe.

Reluctantly 'Cock' followed saying, "This better be good or you will spend the rest of your days here, taking down ceilings".

"Remember that flat you barricaded this morning", said Joe.

"Yes, so what".

"I think there is someone inside", stated Joe, as they made their way down the street.

"How was I to know?" said 'Cock'.

"Did you check before you started", asked Joe.

"No, I was told the flat was empty so I just did as I was told", replied 'Cock'.

"You better get up there as quick as you can before you have a death on your hands", answered Joe. "What sort of an eejit are you to do a stupid thing like that".

They returned to the flat, removed the galvanised iron and, sure enough, inside was an old lady in a state of shock.

"Missus, are you all right" enquired Joe. "Why didn't you call out?"

"I was afraid son", replied the old lady in a nervous voice. "I thought it was the flat opposite. It was only when I tried to open the door that I realised what was wrong.

"Just as well I came back to collect the surplus materials, you could have been here for God only knows when", said Joe glaring at 'Cock Robin' who just stood there with a blank expression on his face.

"Sorry about the trouble caused Missus, will you be alright?", enquired Joe.

"I'll be alright son, as long as I can open and close the door", replied the old lady, who seemed to have recovered from the shock. Turning to 'Cock' he said, "it's a pity you didn't look before you began the barricade".

"You were here too, why didn't you look?", answered 'Cock'.

"Don't try to blame me, I'm only the helper. You are supposed to be the tradesman", said Joe firmly. "We'd better check the other flat before you give a repeat performance.

They searched the other flat and found it to be empty. Using the same materials they barricaded the door and returned to the dug-out to finish lunch.

The moment 'Cock' left to attend to the 'barricaded flat' Billy and the gang immediately made tracks to the vacant house to recover the lead hidden in the basement. With the aid of a wheelbarrow, after first ensuring that a 'look-out' was in place, the booty was quickly moved to the local scrap merchant and exchanged for the going rate. Carefully the money was divided equally between the crew. Even Larry the Nipper got an equal share. By the time 'Cock' returned to the 'dug-out' the business was complete.

Whether the authorities were aware of this illegal practice or not, it certainly could not condone it, with the filthy nature of the work and the terrible conditions. Perhaps it was more prudent to turn a blind eye.

Dave spent a miserable few weeks working on the flying-shores, hating every minute of it. Lunch hour was the worst, having to eat under such awful conditions.

He took to going for walks during lunch-hour, anything to get away from the dugout. On a few occasions he bumped into Larry trying to conceal under his coat a long sash weight, heading no doubt for the scrap yard.

He mentioned it to his two mates. They laughed, saying "Poor old Larry, he's been doing that for ages, gets the price of a cigarette and a match for his trouble".

After the big lead haul things went smoothly for a week or so, till the spoils ran out, with only ceilings to be taken down there was very little opportunity to make extra money. One of the crew with nothing better to do during lunch-hour rambled into one of the vacant houses next for demolition, up the stairs to the first floor window. Looking out at the deserted street below he noticed one of the window shutters ajar. Reaching in he lifted out one of the sash weights. He was a little surprised at the colour. Normally the colour is rust brown, they being made of cast-iron, only this one was a yellow/green colour. Out of curiosity he scratched with a nail only to discover it was made of solid brass. In his excitement he dropped it on his foot but he felt no pain as he raced down the stairs, dragging his leg behind him as he headed for the dugout.

He almost knocked down 'Cock Robin' as he charged in the door crying, "Billy, Billy, where's Billy?"

"Where you should be, working", retorted 'Cock'. "I'll give you one minute to get back to work".

When he found Billy he was out of breath from running. Unable to speak he gestured with his hands.

"What's the matter with you?" asked Billy. "Did you see a ghost or what?" Slowly he regained his voice and blurted out what he had found.

"Brass sash weights, are you mad?" replied Billy. "There is no such thing, you have been working too long with 'Cock Robin', it's beginning to rub off".,

"I'm telling you, they are brass sash weights", he cried, "come and see for yourself".

"All right", answered Billy, "lead the way". Things were so bad at the moment he was prepared to try anything, even something as ridiculous as 'brass sash weights'.

"Where's 'Cock Robin' now?" he asked.

"He's at the other end of the street closing up a vacant flat", came the reply.

"Hope he does a better job than the last one", laughed Billy. "The two of us will take a look". "If the 'Cock' comes along tell him I'm gone to the jacks".

They made their way quickly through the back gardens of the houses and arrived at the appointed house, up the stairs. Sure enough it was confirmed, the weights were indeed solid brass.

"Holy God, these are worth at least a fiver each", said an astonished Billy. They hurriedly searched the house looking for other weights. Too late, all had been removed.

"What became of them", said a shocked voice.

"How do I know", snorted Billy as he searched for an explanation, him being the acknowledged leader had got his eye wiped. It dawned on him. No it couldn't be. He's too dumb to pull a stroke like that, but who else could it have been.

"Larry", they cried in unison. Hadn't they all laughed at him, with the ridiculous sash weights, the price of a cigarette, how are you.

"It was Larry, wait till I get my hands on the little crook", roared Billy, "and to think that we shared our last stroke with him, the miserable creep".

The word spread like wildfire, some were for stringing him up there and then. He had outsmarted them. Each in their hearts knew that, given the same opportunity, they would have done exactly the same.

The City Morgue

"God, I'll never get these timesheets finished", he muttered to himself as the phone rings. "Hello, Civic Maintenance Section, can I help you?".

"Bernard, Jimmy here, what became of the few blocks and the bit of mortar you were to send?", enquired the voice on the phone.

"Listen Jimmy, that bit of stuff was loaded on the truck this morning but the shagging lorry broke down near the Cattle Market", replied an agitated Bernard, "threw the deliveries into a heap".

"What will I do, I can't stand here much longer", answered Jimmy, "yer man is beginning to ask questions".

"Tell him to go and take a running jump at himself", Bernard replied. "You daren't open your mouth here, the man in charge is a quare sort of a fella", said Jimmy.

"It will be with you within the hour", said Bernard with a sigh. It was going to be one of those days.

"I hope so, we'll keep out of the sight in case your man starts ringing up", replied Jimmy.

"Dolan's aul truck broke down again; had to be towed back to the yard with a full load", answered Bernard with a resigned expression in his voice. "You are not the only one left waiting".

"OK, just thought I'd let you know", said Jimmy. "Can't be too careful with some of these people".

"Thanks Jimmy, see you", said Bernard replacing the phone. "God, this place is a right mess all over a bloody truck breaking down. All we need now is an emergency to really screw things up", he said to himself.

Phone rings again. "Not again, it's always the same". Lifting the receiver he asks, "Can I help you?"

A strong articulate voice enquired. "May I speak to the Inspector-in-Charge please?"

"Certainly, may I ask who is calling please", said Bernard.

The voice replied, "The City Coroner's Office".

"One moment please", answered Bernard. "I'll transfer your call". He pressed the necessary buttons and the phone was answered.

"Billy, someone on from the Coroner's Office, sounds very solemn".

"He would, working there, thanks Bernard". "Billy Smith speaking, what can I do for you?"

Again the voice spoke. "I have been informed by the Porter that the drains in the City Morgue have become blocked or choked"".

"How serious is i?t" enquired Billy. "Is it urgent or can it wait?7"

"It is very serious indeed", the voice replied. "The City Coroner is obliged to perform a number of autopsies this very afternoon, it is essential that this matter be attended to immediately".

"Very well", answered Billy. "I'll have it seen to right away".

"Again, I cannot emphasise enough the urgency of this matter", said the voice. "I thank you for your assistance and good morning".

"Good morning to you too", answered Billy who replaced the receiver and left his office to see Bernard.

Bernard was the Depot clerk and general factotum who, in many ways, ran the Depot. Everything ran through him; materials, transport, scaffolding, etc. Answering phones, contacting staff on various jobs, dealing with enquiries from Heads of Departments to General Operatives. If something was required in a hurry, no matter what it be, a few nails, concrete blocks, ladders, he would arrange for it to be delivered without delay. Having contacts in many other Departments he was able to call upon their facilities in times of emergency, a practice frowned upon by most Departments, who preferred to operate as independent units. In each Department there is a Bernard, who keeps the system going but rarely receives credit or recognition except the respect of those who work with them.

"Bernard, an emergency in the Morgue. Where is Peter Hinch working today?" asked Billy.

"He's not, been out sick for a few days", replied Bernard.

"Better get someone else", said Billy. "Is Paddy Duane anywhere handy?"

"He is in Exchange Buildings, fitting a new water heater in the canteen", replied Bernard.

"Get him on the blower as quick as you can", stated Billy.

"Right, he won't be impressed about having to go to the Morgue", answered Bernard.

"That's his hard luck. Like a lot of us he doesn't have much choice", retorted Billy, who turned on his heel, secure in the knowledge that it was in safe hands.

Paddy and his mate Dessie had removed the old heater and were in the process of fitting a new water heater in the staff canteen.

"Dessie, will you hold the end of that pipe while I tighten this nut?" said a red faced Paddy lying on the floor beneath the sink unit.

"Sure I'm only here to serve", replied Dessie, reaching down to lend a hand.

"This bloody heater is slightly different from the one it's replacing", cried Paddy. "You never get the same type, always some adjustments to be made".

"Makes the work more interesting, keeps you on your toes", was Dessie's response. "You might go to seed before your time".

"Imagine anyone going to seed in this place", replied Paddy, "wouldn't get time".

"You never know", said Dessie, "did you see yer man Walsh this morning".

"Walsh, which, ... ah you mean 'Porky' Walsh, the Carpenter, answered Paddy. "He's not going to seed, he just can't get enough drink, that's what's wrong with him".

"Did you see the state of him", enquired Dessie, "looked like something the cat dragged home".

"He always looks like that on Monday morning", replied Paddy. "Never saw him any other way. How he keeps going I'll never know".

"Holy Jaysus, did you see his eyes this morning", said a shocked Dessie, "hope he doesn't come across a mirror in his travels, the shock would be fatal".

"For him or the mirror", answered Paddy.

"Both", replied Dessie.

Paddy was a large, soft jelly baby of a man, easygoing, given to fits of laughter that suited his large frame. When excited, his normal high pitched voice, (reminiscent of Andy Devine), would rise an octave or two, causing heads to turn. Like most tradesmen he came from a family of Plumbers, not one who cared to be hustled, one job at a time was his style.

Paddy's bag was legendary, a large hold-all with extra strong handles, into which everything from his lunch to bits of lead, short copper pipe, washers, brass fittings plus his tools. He could be observed trundling around town going from job to job and always the bag in tow. Every now and then the bag was emptied out, the lead brass and copper was taken to the scrap-yard and traded in for the price of a few pints.

"Get a 310 instantor fitting out of the bag, will you?" said Paddy.

"How you manage to find anything in that bag beats me", replied Dessie. "What do you keep in it, the family jewels?"

"Don't knock that bag, saved me on numerous occasions. I can always find something to take me out of a hole. You name it, it's in the bag".

"Plus anything else you care to mention, Uncle Tom Cobbly and all".

"Uncle who?"

"Never mind, here's the 310".

"Thanks, won't be long now".

"That's what the dog said when the train went over his tail".

"What dog?" asked a confused Paddy.

"It doesn't matter, where are we going next?"

"Pearse Street Library, a leaking cistern in the Ladies".

"But we were there a few weeks ago, is it the same one".

"I don't know. If it is there's not much I can do, I told the Foreman it should be replaced".

"I suppose you got the usual answer".

"How did you guess. Wasn't in the Estimates, has to be ordered, takes weeks and when it does come it won't be the same type, more extra work trying to make it fit".

"Variety is the spice of life".

"It may well be but once, just once for a change, it would be nice to replace something without major alterations to the plumbing system".

"Now you are asking for too much".

Dessie had worked as a plumber's mate for years, serving with a variety of tradesmen. With the experience gained he was almost as good as some of the tradesmen in his own right. It goes without saying that he could never be employed as a plumber, not having served an apprenticeship. He and Paddy were the best of pals, both from the same generation but completely different backgrounds. Paddy a city man, Dessie a county man.

A plumber's mate is more than just for carrying a bag of tools or materials, his assistance is vital given the type of work involved. More times than not two pairs of hands are required, certain shared skills are essential to complete the work.

The telephone rings and keeps ringing.

"Hello, Exchange Buildings, can I help you?"

"Is that you Dave?" asks Bernard.

"Yes, who's that, ah it's you Bernard", said Dave. "Didn't recognise your voice, you sound different".

"It's the swanky voice I use on the phone, you never know who might answer", replied Bernard.

"You could have fooled me", answered Dave. "How's it going, busy?"

"You can say that again", said Bernard. "By the way, how are you fixed for material?"

"I have enough to keep a few Carpenters going for a few days", came the reply.

"Is Paddy Duane anywhere handy?" enquired Bernard.

"Sure, he's just across the way. Hold on and I'll get him", he said, leaving the telephone hanging. "Paddy, you are wanted on the phone".

"Who is it?" answered Paddy in an agitated voice, "can't you see I'm busy".

"It's Bernard of the Yard", Dave replied.

"I don't care if it is Fabian of the Yard", Paddy answered, dragging his not inconsiderable weight from under the sink unit.

"Bernard, you are looking good", he said in his most charming falsetto voice.

"Flattery will get you nowhere", replied Bernard.

"What's up, if it is overtime I'm not available", said Paddy. "I'm going duck shooting in the Wicklow Hills".

"Fuck the ducks", replied Bernard with a laugh. "You know what you can do with the ducks".

"That's not a very refined way of expressing yourself, I'm surprised at you", Paddy answered softly.

"I have a nice little emergency for you", Bernard said just as quietly.

"You have, have you, well it's just going to have to wait till we are finished here".

"It can't wait, must be attended to immediately, if not sooner".

"I don't care if it is the City Manager himself, we have the water turned off here. If we don't get finished, there will be no 'effin' water for lunch".

"This job takes precedence over everything".

"If there is no water here there will be hell to pay and I'm not going to carry the can", replied an agitated Paddy. "Do you realise how many big chiefs there are in this building".

"I don't care how many 'Chiefs or Indians' there are. The City Coroner out ranks them all".

"The City Coroner, but he's responsible for the, ..."

"That's right, you got it in one, the City Morgue", said Bernard with a laugh.

"The Morgue; thank God that's not my area", said a relieved Paddy. "You better get Peter Hinch, he looks after that horrible place".

"That's the problem, he's out sick and you are the only plumber available", replied Bernard.

He could feel the intake of breath, followed by silence.

"Paddy, are you there?", he enquired.

"He's a cute bastard, that fellow, must have got a whisper".

"Cute or not, they have a choke down there, so make tracks", said Bernard, trying to imagine the expression on Paddy's face.

"A choke in the Morgue, you must be joking", said an incredulous Paddy.

"It's no joking matter, they are expecting a consignment of dead bodies this afternoon and the drains have to be cleared before an autopsy can be performed".

"I would hate to disappoint the City Coroner, charming man that he is", said Paddy in his most charming voice, "but without a set of rods what's the point".

"The lorry is already on its way with a set so drop everything and run".

"Bernard, have a heart", pleaded Paddy, "can you not get someone else. I don't think I'd have the stomach for a place like that".

"What do you mean you haven't the stomach; there was not much wrong with your stomach last night and you larraping down pints to a band playing", answered Bernard.

"Ah will you stop for God's sake. I believe it's a terrible kip of a place", said Paddy.

"Not at all, Butlins holiday camp, red coats and all", replied Bernard, beginning to relish the idea of Paddy's dilemma. "You'll have the time of your life, — I like that, the time of your life in the Morgue".

"Don't rub it in, think of the poor unfortunates in the Morgue", replied Paddy.

"I'm sure a few of them would give anything to be able to clear a choke, no matter where it was", Bernard answered. "Anyway, best of luck".

"I know who my friends are", retorted Paddy, "shag you anyway".

Paddy replaces the phone and turns to Dessie.

"Did you hear that, we have to go to the Morgue right away".

"But we are not finished here, what about the staff here", said a puzzled Dessie, "they will have no water".

"That's what I said, I'm not taking the rap for this, it's not my fault", stated Paddy firmly.

"Heard the Morgue is a quare sort of a place", said Dessie, "especially the Porter who works there, he's a head case".

"I don't want to hear another word about it, I'm sick at the very thought", replied a worried Paddy.

"I'll stick a few tools in my pocket, just in case", said a resigned Dessie, "no point in dragging that bag with us. By the way, where are we going to get a set of rods".

"The rods are on their way. Jaysus, another half an hour and we would have been finished here", replied an unhappy plumber.

"A good soldier does what he is told", answered Dessie.

"Sorry Dessie, I suppose you are right", said Paddy.

"We are stuck with it, make the best of it", said Dessie calmly, they both knew they had no choice.

"That's an understatement if ever I heard one, make the best of a choke in the Morgue", said Paddy, trying to put a brave face on it.

"That's some joke alright, only the joke is on us", answered Dessie, "are you ready?".

"I'm not exactly looking forward to this assignment".

"Might be only a wash hand basin or a gully trap that's choked", replied Dessie, trying to reassure his mate, "a few darts of the plunger might do the job".

"I hope so", said Paddy, "ours is not to reason why, etc. etc".

They gathered whatever tools required and headed off, with no great sense of urgency in their step.

"Where exactly is this place?", enquired Paddy.

"Behind the Bus Station in Store Street", answered Dessie.

"Maybe we could slip in for a pint, help to steady the nerves", suggested Paddy.

"Too risky. If you get caught you are down the road with your comic cuts in your hand", replied Dessie, who was just as fond of a pint as anyone but drew the line during working hours.

"Sometimes I wonder would a fella be better off on the labour", said Paddy shaking his head, "especially getting a lousy detail like this".

"We are only small fry at the bottom of the heap", answered Dessie.

"That's for sure", nodded Paddy in agreement.

"Must be nice all the same, to be sitting in a nice comfortable office, out of the wind and rain", mused Dessie, "and you giving orders to everyone. You'd last a lot longer than us".

"It sure beats what we are doing", agreed Paddy.

"A well paid, respectable job", said Dessie.

"Respectable, are you joking", retorted Paddy.

"Compared with us, it is", replied Dessie.

"That's what you think", said an agitated Paddy. "Ours might be considered a dirty job, but it's clean dirt, it can be washed off".

"For Christ's sake, there is no such thing as 'clean dirt', responded Dessie.

"Oh yes there is", insisted Paddy.

"How do you make that out?", asked a puzzled Dessie.

"I'll tell you. Last year we got a choke in one of those swanky offices over there", said Paddy, "where all those 'so-called' respectable people work".

"I wasn't your mate then", replied Dessie.

"No, Peter O'Brien was with me", answered Paddy. "Anyway we arrived with the rods, lifted the manhole cover, and what do you think we found?".

"The usual, I suppose", said Dessie.

"Wrong, I'll tell you what we found. Listen to this, these are our superiors, big shots, who sit in judgement of us, tell us what to do".

"What exactly did you find?" enquired a curious Dessie.

"Condoms! That's what we found", stated Paddy with contempt in his voice.

"Con whats", said a confused Dessie.

"In layman's terms, … 'French Letters'"!.

"No", replied shocked Dessie.

"Oh, but it's true, that's your superiors for you", cried Paddy, raising his fist in anger. "Looking down their noses at us, one step out of line and we are gone".

" You mean to say, they were, …… Oh, you know what!" said a wide-eyed incredulous Dessie.

"What else, they were hardly making balloons out of them", answered Paddy.

"You must have made a mistake; people don't do things like that at work", said an almost speechless Dessie.

"They don't, God bless your innocence", replied Paddy, "and we are left to clean up after them".

Dessie blessed himself. "In the name of the Father, Son and the Holy Ghost, …. Holy God, that's the worst things I ever heard, did you report them?"

"How in the name of Jaysus could you report something like that", said an agitated Paddy, warming to the subject. "What would I say to the Head of the Department? Excuse me Sir, but I would like to draw your attention to the fact that some members of your staff, how can I put it, have been engaged in practices unbecoming of Ladies or Gentlemen during working hours".

"What did you do?" enquired Dessie.

"I'll tell you what we did. We got a shovel and fished them out and we left them on the ground beside the manhole", said Paddy triumphantly.

"That was the right thing to do", agreed Dessie. "Made a show of them, let everyone see the kind of people they really are".

"Somehow or other I don't think it would worry people like that", answered Paddy. "By the way Dessie, have you ever worked in the Morgue?"

"No, but I worked in the abattoir with Jack Kearney", said Dessie, "next best thing".

"You did. What was it like?" said an anxious Paddy.

"Bloody awful in every sense of the word", replied Dessie. "Blood and guts all over the place. I don't know how any one can work in a place like that. You'd need the stomach like a horse; eh, that's funny".

"What's funny?" answered a pale faced Paddy.

"When you consider what they do in the Abattoir", said a smiling Dessie, as he tried to cheer up his mate, aware of Paddy's concern. "If this place is half as bad it will be too much for me", Paddy replied.

Changing the subject Dessie asked, "Paddy, you worked in the Housing Maintenance Department, what was it like?"

"It was all right, the tenants were terrific", replied Paddy, glad of the change of subject, "you were always sure of a cup of tea".

"Don't think I'd like to be working in peoples' houses, not like a real job", answered Dessie.

"You get used to it after a while", said Paddy.

"Wouldn't like working for a woman, not the same as a Foreman", Dessie replied, nodding his head.

"I remember one time working in Cabra. Got a report of a leak in a bathroom, I suppose it's the best place to have a leak, get it", said Paddy, trying to smile but failing, his mind was elsewhere, "anyway, we checked everywhere; the cistern, the overflow, the pan, the lot, but could find nothing".

"The woman must have been dreaming", suggested Dessie.

"When we came downstairs the woman said and I quote": "Well did you find anything, just look at the ceiling in the kitchen, it's destroyed with watermarks". "Missus", I said, "there is nothing wrong with the toilet"; "there must be", she insisted; "it's just that someone had a bad shot".

"I'm sure that took the wind out of her sails", replied Dessie.

"It certainly did. You should have seen the look on her face, didn't know which way to look", said Paddy. "Next time she will think twice before making a complaint.

"What did she say", enquired Dessie.

"Not a 'Dicky Bird' out of her", answered Paddy. "By the way, you were saying the Porter down here is a head case".

"He sure is. Anyone who worked in a place like that would want to be soft in the head", Dessie said.

"What exactly does he do?" asked Paddy carefully.

"He opens up the bodies so that the Coroner can perform an autopsy", stated Dessie firmly.

"You mean to say, he opens up the remains of some poor bastard, as part of his job", replied Dessie.

Paddy was listening very carefully, trying to imagine what the Morgue was like. He had visions of a place with rivers of blood and a half-crazed man up to his knees in the entrails of some poor unfortunate being just like an old 'Vincent Price' picture, only for real. The nearer they got to Store Street the more apprehensive he became. Having worked all his life as a Plumber, with a vast experience in every aspect of the trade, the Morgue was well out of the normal run of things.

Down the Quays, over Butt Bridge, passing under the 'Loopline' Bridge and into Store Street. As they approached the red-bricked building that was the Morgue Paddy slowed down, leaving Dessie to knock on the door. Paddy waited on the pavement looking decidedly uncomfortable. No reply, he knocks again and still no reply.

"Maybe it's a false alarm", said Paddy hopefully.

"There's another entrance in Amiens Street, behind the pub", replied Dessie, "we'd better give it a try".

The large double gates were standing wide open as they walked into the open yard, Dessie in the lead, Paddy followed reluctantly.

"The right man in the right place", said a booming voice through an open door that stopped them in their tracks. They were confronted by a large burly red faced man, wearing a blood-stained apron, Wellington boots and a white cap, the Porter.

"Now I know what Bernard meant when he said 'Redcoats'", said Paddy.

"What's that you said?", asked the Porter quickly.

"Nothing, nothing, just talking to myself; what seems to be the problem".

"The whole place is choked up and we are expecting a few bodies this afternoon", the Porter explained, realising from the tone of Paddy's voice that he was unhappy to be in the Morgue.

The Porter's job is a very unusual one. He has to prepare any corpse that requires an autopsy, necessitating the opening up of the remains and closing up when the Coroner has completed his examination. There are times when the place is drenched in blood but it never seemed to bother the Porter. When you consider the condition of some of the remains that are taken to the Morgue, he must have a strong stomach indeed.

"What caused the problem?" enquired Paddy.

"Don't ask me, I only work here", said the Porter, "the drains have to be cleared before the Coroner arrives".

"Just show us where the problem is so that we can get away from here as fast as possible", replied Paddy sharply.

"Just follow me", said the Porter as he walked through the open door.

They found themselves in a large hall covered from floor to ceiling with white glazed tiles, three altar type marble tables stood in the centre, the clear outline of a corpse visible beneath a white sheet.

"Don't take any notice of yer man under the sheet", said the Porter in an off-hand manner, "he's quite harmless"; enjoying himself at Paddy's expense.

"The last thing I want to see is the mutilated remains of some poor bastard after being fished out of the Liffey", retorted Paddy.

"Actually, it was out of the Canal, near Croke Park", answered the Porter".Christ, what difference does it make?", snapped Paddy, "just leave well enough alone".

"The drains have backed up from the manhole in the yard", stated the Porter, pointing to the manhole cover in the yard.

Paddy examined the marble tables to ascertain how it worked. Each table had its own internal plumbing system that discharged into the existing drains; he quickly understood where the problem lay.

Paddy announced, "the problem is in the manhole".

"I told you that", replied the Porter loudly.

"I'm the tradesman here, not you", said Paddy sharply, trying to assert his authority.

"All right, don't get a nose on you, I was only trying to help", answered the Porter. "By the way a set of rods were dropped in a few minutes before youse arrived".

"Dessie, see if you can get the lid off the manhole so that we can get out of this weird place", asked Paddy.

Dessie tried to lift the cover but was unable, it was a heavy duty cover. Turning to the Porter he said, "Have you got a shovel or a bar to try and get this cover off?"

"I'll get a shovel from the stores", replied the Porter with a smirk on his face". "Keep an eye on yer man in there in case he tries to run away", looking at Paddy out of the corner of his eye.

Paddy was trying to put a brave face on it. Ignoring the remarks, shifting his not considerable weight from side to side, wishing he was somewhere else.

"Dessie, did you ever see anything like it in your life, the Chamber of Horrors?", said Paddy.

"I didn't believe the stories about your man, not until now", replied Dessie.

It seemed like an eternity before the Porter returned with the shovel.

"Here you are", said the Porter.

"Thanks", answered Dessie.

"Any luck", asked Paddy.

"Yes, it's starting to move", leaning back on the shovel.

"Careful, you are nearly there, don't under any circumstances attempt to put your hand near the cover", warned Paddy, "you could lose a finger".

When the heavy cover was finally raised the manhole was full to the brim and the contents were indescribable, and the smell, ouch. Paddy gave a deep sigh and slowly slumped to the ground, out cold. Dessie looked up just as his mate hit the ground and in trying to grab Paddy he dropped the cover, which crashed back into place, causing it to drench them with the contents of the manhole.

"Holy God", cried Dessie as he turned to where Paddy was stretched out on the concrete yard. "Paddy, are you all right?"

"He collapsed", said the Porter, "I wonder why".

"I don't blame him at the sight and smell of that, I don't feel too good myself", answered Dessie, reaching down to assist Paddy.

"We had better get him inside out of this mess before he catches his end of cold", said the Porter.

"What do you mean inside, not into the Chamber of Horrors", cried Dessie, appalled at the thought.

"Where else, we can't leave him here like that", suggested the Porter. "Holy God, what a smell, our clothes are ruined", said Dessie, looking down at the condition of his clothes.

"I don't know if it was the sight or the smell that done him", replied the Porter.

"Can we carry him into the office", asked Dessie, concerned that Paddy had not moved.

"There's no room in the office. Besides the office staff would object to the smell", replied the Porter.

"Isn't that a pity about the office staff", cried Dessie, angry at the Porter's response, "what about Paddy lying on the ground".

"Look, just take his legs, I'll take this end", said the Porter.

"I still think it's not right to take him in there with dead bodies all over the place", answered Dessie quietly.

"There is only one at the moment .... he's very heavy, has he lead in his pockets or what?" asked the Porter.

"Where are you going to put him?" enquired Dessie.

"Over there on one of the empty slabs, where else", said the Porter.

With much struggling they somehow managed to haul the limp heavy Paddy into the Morgue where he was stretched out on the cold slab.

"I'll go and get a glass of water", said a distressed Dessie, "try to bring him round".

"There is a cup beside the sink", replied the Porter.

Dessie rushed out to the sink and when he returned with the water he found that the Porter had covered Paddy with a white sheet.

"In case he gets a chill", said the Porter with a grin on his face.

"That's not very funny", cried Dessie, "when he come to you are liable to have another body on your hands".

"Serves him right, a grown man acting like that", replied the Porter. "If he only saw some of the bodies I get in here he would have something to worry about".

"Just the same, we are not all like you. Some of us are a bit sensitive to bodies, especially dead ones", answered Dessie.

"Ah, for God's sake, we all have to die sometime", said the Porter.

"There is a time and place for everything", replies Dessie, "and this is neither the time nor the place to be having fun at someone else's expense".

"He's starting to move, he's coming round", said the Porter.

From beneath the sheet came a low moan, followed by a shriek. The sheet was ripped off by a white faced Paddy, his eyes sticking out like organ stops, and he went out the door like a flash.

"Paddy, come back", shouted Dessie, as the large figure disappeared out of sight.

"He went out that door like a bat out of hell", roared the Porter with laughter, "couldn't see his arse for dust".

Dessie ran across the yard in pursuit but it was too late.

"It's no use, he's gone", said a breathless Dessie, "hope he is all right".

"Can't be much wrong with someone who can run like that", laughed the Porter. "For a fat man he sure can move, that's the funniest thing I've seen in years".

"Give me the rods", snapped Dessie, "so that I can go and see if he is all right".

"OK, here they are", said the still laughing Porter.

"When I get a lift on the cover you stick the handle of the brush under the lid", said Dessie, "are you ready?"

"Right, here we go, I'm ready", said the Porter.

"Yes, I got it, it's safe", answered Dessie, holding the head of the shovel under the manhole cover, rolling it over, out of the way.

"Heavens, what a sight, I've never seen anything like it in my life".

Dessie got out the rods with the plunger in place and began the messy job of clearing the disgusting contents of the manhole. It took time and patience to clear. Once it started to move it went with a roar, leaving the remains to be hosed down.

After hosing down the manhole he washed his own hands and cleaned the rods, tied them together, before replacing the cover.

"Have you a phone here?" he asked the still smiling Porter. "I want to notify the Yard".

"There's a phone in the office, come on, I'll show you", he said, leading the way to a small office, "have you got the number".

"Yes", replied Dessie, dialling the number. "Bernard, Dessie here".

"Well, how did you get on?" enquired Bernard.

"A very messy affair", he replied, "but we got it away".

"How about Paddy, he wasn't impressed about going to the Morgue", said Bernard.

"He conked out in the yard and then scarpered", answered Dessie.

"He what!", came the reply.

"He passed out when we lifted the manhole cover".

"Paddy fainted, you're joking".

"True as God, hope he is alright", said Dessie, "anyway it's time for lunch, see you in the yard".

"Maybe Paddy will be there" replied Bernard, feeling the concern in Dessie's voice.

"Somehow or other I don't think Paddy will be having lunch today".

A group of voluntary workers who assisted in the restoration of Kilmainham Gaol (courtesy of kilmainham Gaol Museum)

Tin Roof Blues

It was another lousy, cold morning, that dreadful, persistent east wind that had settled on the city remained. The men arrived for work, frozen with the cold. It was everywhere, dressed in an assortment of heavy clothes, boots and many forms of headgear. Even the galvanised iron hut that served as a canteen store was inviting, anything to get away from that wind. Framed in the door was the Foreman, whistle in one hand and a note-book in the other, roll -call was due. The ice crunched underfoot like broken glass as each man rushed to be in before the whistle blew.

Inside the yellow glow of the gas lamps spread its light on the faces of the crew, giving a strange, death-like appearance to those present. The air was filled with a mixture of steam and smoke, the babble of voices livened up the otherwise dreary place. Beads of condensation began to form on the cold surface of the galvanised iron roof before dropping indiscriminately on the heads of the assembled crew. Not that anyone notices, they were only too well accustomed to the conditions that pertained, the sieve-like roof offered them only minimum protection from the elements.

The Foreman gave a cough to clear his throat before sounding his whistle to announce roll-call. As each name was called cries of "here", "yes", "anseo" were heard as each of those present replied. "Paddy Kelly". No reply. He repeated, "Paddy Kelly". Again no response.

"He's coming across the yard", said Lesso, one of the carpenters.

"He's not here to answer for himself", replied the Foreman firmly.

"But you can see him coming, look there he is", cried Leslie. "Paddy, hurry up or you will be late".

"And late he is", announced the Foreman, striking a line through his name.

"That's not fair, can't you see him trying to run", answered Lesso, with annoyance in his voice.

"Maybe you would like to swap places with him", enquired the Foreman with a leer on his face. "I can just as easy stop the half-hour's pay on you instead".

The long, dishevelled figure of Paddy Kelly came sliding through the door, almost knocking the foreman over, his matted fair hair scattered in the wind, his blood-shot eyes staring into space. He slumped on a stool, breathless, his hunched shoulders heaved in an effort to replenish his smoke filled lungs.

"You can take your time, you're late", said the Foreman.

It fell on deaf ears. Paddy was too preoccupied to notice. With his lifestyle, running was something he was incapable of. He raised his unfortunate head to reply but to no avail. The look of desperation on his well-worn face sent shock waves through those close enough to see. The distress caused by his efforts reflected the evidence of a life spent abusing mind and body with drink and cigarettes. He was wearing an open necked shirt, a threadbare jumper that offered little protection from the harsh weather, his well worn shoes sadly in need of repair. It was said of him that he was a drinking pal of Brendan Behan: whatever the truth may have been he certainly looked the part.

"Anyone got a light?", he finally said in a hoarse, gravely voice that came from the soles of his feet. In a blaze of light and smoke he drew back his head and dragged the nicotine into his hard pressed lungs.

His fellow carpenters had a great deal of sympathy for him, an understanding of his weakness. They may not have approved of his way of life; at the same time who were they to sit in judgement. When sober Paddy was a likeable, well read man capable of speaking on a variety of subjects, especially politics, a subject not too dear to the hearts of his colleagues. On his bad days, which were becoming all too frequent, he was like something left out in the rain for a month.

"Anyone going to work today", said the Foreman, drawing attention to himself by banging his hand on the table, causing the mugs and cups to jump with fright. "If you are not out of here in 10 seconds, I'll start docking time".

Paddy, who was sitting with his head cradled in his hands, trying to get relief, closed his eyes with shock before giving the Foreman a look that should have turned him into stone.

An air of gloom descended on the men. It was with great reluctance that they began to move, unsuitable as the hut was, at least the heat generated by twenty or so carpenters was preferable to another day spent working outdoors.

"Are the painters working today?" asked Jim Burke, the Shop Steward.

"How do I know?" replied the Foreman. "I'm not in charge of Painters".

"This is a ridiculous situation. They can sit all day in their hut without loss of pay while we have to go out in the freezing cold and rain", answered Jim angrily.

"Don't look at me, all I heard was that it was too cold to paint", replied the Foreman sensing trouble.

"That's marvellous, it's too cold to paint, yet we are expected to repair gutters that are frozen solid with ice", retorted Jim, warming to the subject. "What are we paying, 'wet-time' stamps for anyway?"

"You'd better take it up with your Union", answered the Foreman. "I'm only obeying orders".

"That's what the 'Gestapo' said after the War", replied Jim, feeling he was getting the upper hand in the argument.

The last thing the Foreman needed was a dispute on his job while acting as a temporary Foreman. To have a strike would almost certainly ruin his chances of a permanent appointment.

"Are youse going to work or not?", he cried impatiently.

Some of the older men began to move. At their stage in life, to be working at all was a bonus. Having worked a lifetime on building sites under awful working conditions for some heartless builders, cold was the least of their worries. The younger men were more inclined to question the order of things, as is their want. They were not prepared to accept whatever was dished out to them. The 'lucky to be working' attitude of the older men was not acceptable.

"It's about time this thing was sorted out, once and for all", said an angry Jim, conscious of the support he could feel. "Have you any idea what it's like standing on a ladder for hours on end with the wind blowing up the legs of your trousers?

"Why don't you put your trousers down your stockings", replied the Foreman, trying to make fun of the situation in an effort to divert attention.

"Very funny", said Jim. "It's all right for you, you are not out there in the cold. You won't find many 'brass monkeys' out there and, if you do, they will be eligible to join the 'Luton Girls' Choir'".

"For the last time", said the Foreman trying to assert his authority, "that includes you Paddy Kelly, move it".

In the immortal words of 'Sam Goldwyn' "include me out", replied Paddy who remained seated, still puffing the remains of the cigarette. "Remember you docked a half-hour's pay on me so I won't be starting til 9 o'clock".

At this stage the Foreman was getting purple in the face, confronted by such insubordination, seeing his position being undermined, out of his control: still no one moved.

"Holy god, the Inspector just arrived", came a cry from outside the hut.

It was the last thing on earth the Foreman needed and him with a mutiny on his hands.

"What does hungry head want this hour of the morning", said Jim quickly. "Has he no home to go to - this might be the time to sort out this once and for all".

"Will you keep your mouth shut for Jaysus sake or we will all be sacked", replied the Foreman in desperation.

A terrible silence descended on the crew. It was as if the "Grim Reaper" himself was visited upon them. He was feared by all, having a reputation for being ruthless. He would brook no interference from anyone he perceived as trying to usurp his authority. He bounded in the door, his hard face matched the coldness of the morning, to be greeted by an equally stone-faced crew, and the distrust of each other was clearly evident. His eyes focused on the figure of Paddy Kelly, who true to form, remained seated, ignoring the Inspector's presence.

"And what may I ask is this", he barked, in his usual manner, "a sit down strike?".

"Are you addressing me?" Paddy said calmly.

"No, the fella behind you", answered the Inspector sarcastically, not accustomed to his authority being called into question. No-one moved, not a sound except heavy breathing that came in short bursts, waiting for something to happen, fearing the worst.

"Please acquaint our friend here of the situation that pertains", said Paddy addressing the Foreman and ignoring the Inspector again.

"He was late so I docked him a half-hour's pay", replied the Foreman, regaining some of his confidence in the present of the Inspector.

"Excellent, I could not have done better myself", came the Inspector's cheery response, "for a moment I thought I would have to exercise my authority".

"You're good at that", whispered a voice from the back of the hut. "You're only a 'bollocks'".

The use of such language was commonplace, never at an Inspector. To some it was like swearing at God himself. There was no contact between the workers and the Inspector except for disciplinary reasons. Even then it was channelled through the Foreman or a Union representative. Mutual distrust, bordering on hate, a permanent state of guerrilla warfare existed. For anyone to question his authority was unheard of. The older men, with a few exceptions, lived in fear of this authoritarian regime, having served a long apprenticeship under similar working conditions for numerous building contractors. The younger men, from a more enlightened time, refused to accept the unquestioning acceptance of the 'Status Quo', constantly making representation through their Union to improve their working conditions.

The stone faced Inspector glared at an equally stone faced crew, searching for the face behind the voice, no doubt promising himself to make an example of the culprit. A long silence, broken only by the striking of a match. Paddy Kelly, still seated, lit another cigarette. He began blowing smoke rings that floated gently upwards expertly filling each ring with a smaller one. Fascinated eyes followed them 'til they dissipated on making contact with the galvanised iron roof.

The uneasy silence was broken by the Inspector who announced sharply, "as of now this job is finished". With that he turned on his heel and, beckoning to the Foreman, left the hut. It was like a hand grenade had been placed on the table. For a second no-one moved, then everyone began to talk.

"You have no right to use such bad language, even if you don't like him", cried John, an older carpenter. "I hope you are satisfied".

"That's what has him the way he is", retorted Lesso, a young Carpenter. "Youse are like a lot of sheep".

"All very well for you. Where's an old fella like me going to get a job", said John, annoyed t the attitude of the younger men.

"It's creepy crawlies like you that spoils a job", replied Lesso quickly.

"Hold on now", said Jim Burke, "let's not fight among ourselves. The thing to do is contact the Union before we start blaming each other".

"A lot of good that will do", answered John. "What's the point, it's too late now".

"It's never too late if we stick together", said Jim, trying to diffuse the situation. "Don't panic, I'll go and ring the Union; anyone got any change?"

The Foreman returned with a smirk on his round face and with the echo of the departing Inspector's car in his ear.

"I have some good news and some bad news", he said triumphantly. "Which do you want first?"

"We've had enough bad news for one day, it will be a change to get some good news", answered Jim, anxious to hear.

"The good news is a new job is starting in town", he replied. "The bad news for you is, I'll be in charge".

The news was greeted with a general sigh of relief. After having endured weeks of dreadful hardship repairing gutters in the coldest Winter in years, the prospect of indoor work appealed to everyone.

"I never want to see a gutter again", cried a delighted Jim, slapping Paddy Kelly on the back, causing Paddy to almost choke on the cigarette he was smoking.

"For Jaysus sake will you stop", coughed Paddy as he endeavoured to rescue the faithful cigarette from his throat. "What are you trying to do, kill me?"

"It would take more than that to kill me", replied Jim. The good die young. Where's the job anyway?"

"In Blackhall Place", answered the Foreman, happy to be retained in his supervisory role.

"Where's the Depot in Blackhall Place", enquired Jim.

"A yard near Benburb Street, the work will be around Church Street", answered the Foreman. "A lorry will be here shortly to collect the tools and any other gear".

"How do we get there?" said Jim.

"Walk", replied the Foreman.

"You're not serious", answered Jim in disbelief.

"I'm perfectly serious, what do you expect, a luxury coach?" he retorted sarcastically.

"You mean we have to walk from Crumlin to Blackhall Place today, in that weather", said an incredulous Jim.

"You can do as you like", he replied. "Take the bus, or if you are feeling flush, a taxi, that's your problem".

"What about the bus fare?" enquired Jim, trying to extract some concession. "We can put it on our timesheets".

"You can put what you like on your timesheet", answered the Foreman, "but you won't get paid".

"That will take hours", replied Jim who had no intention of paying his fare during working hours without compensation. "You can expect us when you see us".

"Don't worry, I'll be waiting", said the Foreman.

"Now listen to this", announced Jim in a loud voice, "we are going to another job in town and as no provision has been made to transport us, as of now we are on 'walking time' and I don't want any defectors either".

Leading the way like a latter day 'Pied Piper', heads bent in the cold morning air, Jim headed off in the company of the younger, more militant ones. The older men were more circumspect, hardship, they had spent a lifetime labouring under its yoke, but not having a choice. While agreeing in principle with a 'walking protest' they were not going to impose further hardship on themselves, even the wrath of their workmates was preferable to that.

Before the leading bunch was out of sight, leaving the back markers free to take a bus, not for them a long walk into town, hardship they had endured enough of it. The weather deteriorated, flakes of sleet began falling, adding to the underfoot conditions and the discomfort of the 'walking martyrs' as they slowly edged their way to town. Turning onto the Quays at Kingsbridge, they were met with a shower of hailstones that whipped at their faces, stinging like bees. Out in front Jim lead by example, forcing the others to hang on with assurances that at least, some shelter was to be provided. Crossing a windswept Watling Street Bridge, they finally reached Blackhall Place famished with the cold and hunger, the cold etched on their pale faces. A parked lorry outside the entrance to the yard was being unloaded of materials and numerous tool boxes. Reaching the gate first, Jim stepped in to survey the 'promised land', the others followed in anticipation.

They were met by the Inspector and the Foreman, who stood in the centre of an opensided hay barn, with the elements pouring in on them. It was like something out of 'Dickens' or the middle ages, an empty yard littered with rubbish, concrete blocks and the best of weeds.

"Holy God", cried Jim, appalled at what he saw. "You call that a depot, you wouldn't put pigs in a place like that, never mind tradesmen".

"Some work is required to make it suitable", replied the Inspector sharply, unaccustomed to his judgement being called into question.

"If you think we are going to accept working conditions like that, you have another think coming", answered Jim, turning on his heel and followed by the other men, retiring to the pavement outside.

"Where do you think you are going?", asked a surprised Inspector. The Foreman remained quiet. His position was to implement the directions of his superior, not to question them, whatever his feelings were, silence was for him the preferred option.

"You have a hard neck, expecting us to work under such conditions", reported Jim.

"Anything you have to say you can say it to the Union delegate".

"It's a temporary measure", said a stern faced Inspector, "are you refusing to work?"

"No comment", answered Jim, "that's for the Union to decide, the delegate will be here within the hour". "You do realise the consequences of your actions", stated the Inspector firmly. "I can have you all suspended without pay for refusing to work".

By this time all the crew had arrived. They gathered outside to await developments. There was no question of breaking ranks, even the most fainthearted and docile realised it was time to make a stand. An agitated Inspector paced up and down, glaring at the men outside on the pavement, glancing at his watch in annoyance. The Foreman was making himself busy with the unloading of the truck.

After what seemed an eternity, the delegate arrived going straight to Jim, who in no uncertain terms acquainted him with the situation and of the men's feelings. Inside, the Inspector and Foreman were in deep conversation, only too well aware of the delegate's presence. The delegate, with Jim in tow, walked into the yard to inspect the place for himself. The Inspector quickly crossed the yard to meet him. At the entrance the crew watched, hoping for a view of the confrontation about to take place.

"I hope he calls a strike", said Lesso, in anticipation.

"Less of that kind of talk", said John, an experienced and wiser man. "Last time we went on strike we were left out for six months and what did we gain, nothing, a reduction in pay".

A long and lean faced man, a pipe permanently projecting from the side of a hard mouth, flat cap well pulled down, concealed a keen pair of green eyes. Quietly he would sit, saying very little, but observing everything. Traces of air hair peeped out from beneath the cap. Was he baldy, a question often asked in his absence. Some said he was, others disagreed, no one dared ask, or worse, removing the cap, he was not a man to trifle with.

"That was years ago", replied Lesso, who regarded anyone who advocated consultation as a means of resolving disputes, a coward". What about getting on to the newspapers to highlight our grievance, that would certainly shake them up".

"I'm sure the Union will come to some agreement that will satisfy everyone", answered John, anxious to avoid industrial action". "It's not worth being at the loss of a few week's pay".

"Put the boot in, show them who's Boss", said Lesso quickly, "he needs to be taught a lesson".

Short in stature, with a fine head of black curly hair, quick witted and as sharp as a tack, a real street-wise young man. Neatly dressed, like his father before, who, as a 'Jazzer' in his day, a touch of vanity prevented him wearing glasses, thought it would spoil his appearance.

The group of four was gathered in some strong and heated debate, with much waving and pointing of hands, each in their turn, stating their positions. The spectators followed every gesture with keen interest. The debate swayed to and fro, till finally an agreement was achieved.

The Inspector left in a great flurry of business, his face not displaying any emotion or feelings of how the meeting went, or if any decisions had been taken.

Jim gestured to the waiting crew, anxious to hear what were the proposals for resolving the dispute.

"Now listen carefully", said a tired Jim, "we have persuaded them to make this place habitable".

"It would be easier to burn it down", chipped in Lesso.

"They are making available timber and galvanised iron to close off the open side of the shed", replied Jim. "As soon as the materials arrive we can start making this place like home".

"Some home, what about a 'Jacks'?" enquired the ever present Lesso.

"A new one is being organised right away", answered Jim. "In the meantime, if you are short-taken you'll have to make do with the public toilets in the Markets".

"I'll never make it", laughed Lesso, "it's too far".

"In that case you'd better stay outside and down wind", replied Jim.

"What about making tea, I'm dying for a cup", said John slowly. "Organise your 'Billy cans' and get a fire going", said Jim. "I could do with a hot drink myself".

Jim thanked the delegate for his prompt action and promised to keep him informed of any further developments. The delegate left, satisfied that a dispute had been settled to everyone's satisfaction, a strike was the result of a failure by both sides in a dispute situation to resolve their differences from which no-one benefited.

In the absence of the Inspector there was a more relaxed air about the place and in no time a fire was blazing in the coke brazier. A square of perforated metal was placed on the brazier and with great skill and ingenuity, the many 'Billy cans' were placed to boil. The warm fire was surrounded and supervised by a freezing group of men, anxious to partake of some heart-warming drinks. It had been a long and cold day, the heat from the fire was reflected in their thawing faces.

By the time the truck returned with the necessary materials it was a far happier crew that immediately set about closing off the open side of the shed. As daylight began to fail the last nail was driven home much to the relief of all concerned, the obligatory whistle sounding 'Reveille' brought an end to the day.

Next morning saw little change in the weather, if anything it was colder, a heavy frost overnight covered everything with a thin white layer of frost. The men began to arrive in ones and twos, picking their way carefully through the ice filled snow that lay on the ground. Gathering inside, inching their way as close as possible to the glowing fire, their outstretched hands trying to soak up the heat. Even Paddy Kelly had managed to put in an appearance before roll-call, looking very fresh and in fine form.

"Paddy, you are looking very spruce this cold morning", said Lesso, "did you go home at all last night?"

"I most certainly did", replied Paddy with a jaunt in his voice, "and why wouldn't I, working beside the Markets".

"What's so special about the Markets?", asked a puzzled Lesso.

"My dear young man", answered Paddy in a majestic voice, "working here I'm surrounded by many 7 o'clock houses, what more could a poor soul require?"

"If I catch anyone in a pub it's down the road you'll go", interrupted the Foreman, "it's time to get this show on the road".

As each name was called out a work docket was handed to each in their turn, detailing the work to be carried out in each house. After studying the docket and depending on the work to be done, collected some materials, sash cords, window or door fittings from the store.

Out onto the street, tool boxes in tow, they carefully threaded their way over the ice-packed road in the direction of Church Street with no great sense of urgency, across the open space that is Smithfield, single file, like sheep going through a gap, before reaching the protective wall on the old Distillery. As they turned into Church Street the familiar figure of Paddy Kelly crossed the street.

"Where's Paddy heading for?" enquired Lesso.

"He's heading for the public toilets in the Markets", answered Jim, with a twinkle in his eye.

"Ask a silly question. If you believe that you will believe anything", replied Lesso.

"That's what he said, who am I to call him a liar", said Jim.

"If your man catches him, he's gone", warned Lesso.

"Paddy knows how to look after himself", replied Jim with a grimace.

They descended without warning or prior notice on an unsuspecting terrace of single-storey cottages, situated between Church Street and Beresford Street, mainly occupied by elderly people, mostly widows. Not a sign of life appeared in the close curtained windows, not surprising considering the weather. Each of them took up position outside their respective house. With great reluctance gently knocking on the door "with a sponge", said Jim, not too anxious to invade the privacy of the old people at such an ungodly hour. Within minutes the Inspector appeared with the Foreman in tow and he began banging on each door demanding access, so that work could commence.

Locked doors were opened slowly by terrified old people unaccustomed to such an early and unwelcome intrusion.

"What's wrong son", enquired a frightened old lady who peeped out from behind the heavy door, a woollen blanket wrapped around her small shoulders, "you put the fear of God in me".

"It's the Corpo, Missus", said Jim quietly, reading the concern expressed in her eyes, "we have to do some repairs to your house".

"What repairs son?" replied the old lady, "I didn't report anything".

"We have to carry out necessary repairs before the painters come".

"You'd better come in son out of the cold", said the old lady opening the door to admit him.

"Thanks Missus, once the door is closed yer man will clear off", he said.

Closing the door behind him left him in complete darkness.

"Missus, will you switch on the light please. I can't see a thing", asked a concerned Jim, feeling along the wall for a light switch.

"I've no electricity son", said the old lady, "it was cut off".

"How do you manage without light?", he enquired, still lost in the darkness.

"I use an oil lamp. Lucky for me I didn't throw it out when the electric came", she replied without a trace of bitterness in her voice, "couldn't afford to pay. Would you like a cup of tea".

The old lady expertly got the lamp going. It threw light on a sparsely furnished room. The air was filled with the smell of carbolic soap, a sink in one corner beside the window and a gas cooker in the other.

"I wouldn't impose on you, Missus", answered Jim, "thanks just the same".

"It's no trouble, it will only take a few minutes to light the fire", she replied, "the gas is cut off too".

"You will do no such thing, Missus", said Jim, appalled to hear that in this day and age anyone would be without such basic services.

"What exactly are you going to do son?" she enquired.

"I have to fit a new back door and a few sash cords", he replied.

"A new back door, very swanky indeed", she answered cheerfully, "wait till I tell me next door neighbour, she'll be as jealous as hell".

"She sure will Missus. Now, when I take down the old door it's going to be cold in here", he said. "I suggest that you go into the other room 'till its finished".

"You're right son, I'll go and get dressed and light the fire", she replied. "By the way, what do you do with the old door son?"

"Usually they are taken back to the Depot for firewood", he answered, "why?"

"I was only wondering, wouldn't say no to a few bits of wood", she said quietly.

"Tell you what, Missus", he said, detecting a note of desperation in her voice, "when the door is down I'll cut it into firewood for you".

"Oh no son, it might cost you your job", she said in fear, "a few pieces of wood will do".

"Just leave it to me, Missus", he replied, "it's a sad day if you can't have a few pieces of wood for a fire".

"God bless you son", she answered.

The old lady left the room and he began the task of taking down the door in preparation for the new door. With the door down he removed the furniture, hinges, locks, bolts and the weather board that were to be reused. A loud knock on the hall door. "Not the Inspector again", he thought to himself. With a resigned sigh he opened the door to find the bold Lesso standing waiting for him.

"Come on, it's time for hot drinks", he said, "you don't want to be late, twice the same day".

"Give me a minute to put away my tools", replied Jim. "Missus, are you there?"

"Yes son", came her answer.

"I'm going for a cup of tea, I'll be back in about 20 minutes", said Jim.

"That's all right. Tell you what, here's a key, I won't be here when you come back", she said, "I always go to 10 o'clock Mass".

"Thanks Missus, see you later".

They rambled off to the Depot in the company of the others in time for a badly needed cup of tea.

"We thought we were badly off", said Lesso, "the poor old woman where I am has neither gas or electric, they were cut off".

"Same with me", replied John.

A few others had similar tales to tell.

"They call this a Christian country", said John with a trace of irony in his voice, "and they leave old people without basic services".

"The strange thing is they all go to Mass every day", said Lesso, not renowned for his religious fervour.

"Don't blame the Church for that", interrupted John, a staunch defender of the faith, "they don't run the country".

"Are you kidding", replied Lesso, "you can't fart in this town without them knowing about it".

"We don't want to know either", answered John quickly.

"Just the same, it's not right to cut off gas and electric from old people", said Lesso.

"I couldn't agree more, no use blaming the Church though", said John.

"I'm sure the only reason they go each morning is to get out of the cold for an hour or so", Lesso retorted.

"What would you know about the inside of a Church anyway? When was the last time you were inside one?" asked John.

"None of your bloody business. Just because you go to Mass doesn't make you any better than me", snapped Lesso. "A lot of crawthumpers and hypocrites".

"We'll have none of that kind of talk on my job", interjected the Foreman, "it's back to work time".

There was no great rush to return to work, asking for screws, nails, any excuse to postpone the inevitable. Eventually they left, leaving the Foreman to organise whatever materials were required. The labourer loaded the hand cart and suitably laden, headed off having been advised to be back as soon as possible, not to hang about and, more important, "keep away from the 'Bookies' in case your man pays a surprise visit".

The Foreman well understood how the system operated, having served in a supervisory position and as a carpenter on many similar type jobs. All bets were given to the labourer at tea-break and him being an old hand, discreetly went about the business of laying bets.

"Anyone see Paddy Kelly?" asked Lesso as they made their way back to Church Street.

"There was a sighting around 10 o'clock", said John, "he was working next door to me, where he is now is anyone's guess".

"He's a terrible man. One of these days he'll get caught", replied Jim.

"It's the worst possible place for him to be working, with a pub on every corner", answered Lesso, who had a soft spot for Paddy, "and they open from 7 o'clock in the morning".

"Paddy's no fool, he's long enough at the game to get caught", said John, more in hope than anything else.

"The cutest hen lays out", Jim replied, "anyway see you all at lunch hour".

They broke up, each going to their separate dwelling. Jim knocked on the door before turning the key and resuming work on the door. Shortly afterwards the new door was delivered, no sign of the lady of the house. He wasted no time in hanging and fitting the door. On a cold morning there is no better way to get the circulation going than hanging a door. He worked away replacing locks and fittings till they were in place before turning his attention to the old door, reducing it to firewood in no time. In neat bundles he laid them out beside the now dead fireplace. The time slipped away before he realised it was 12.45, time to pack up the tools and make tracks. Being so engaged he never noticed if the old lady had returned.

Before leaving he knocked on the bedroom door to let her know he was off. Getting no response, he hesitated, "must have went to the shops", he thought to himself. Still, something suggested he should perhaps open the door. "No, it would be an invasion of her privacy". After all, he had been welcomed into her home. He opened the hall door. Better hurry or he would be late for lunch. As Shop Steward, he had to set an example for the others.

The blank bedroom door stared back at him, as if daring him.

"I'd better check, just in case", he said to himself.

Opening the door, after first knocking, he peered into the darkened room, a small chest of drawers and a single bed filled the small room. Fast asleep on the bed, fully clothed, was the old lady, her grey hair scattered on the pillow.

"Missus, I'm off for my lunch", he said quietly, not wishing to disturb or frighten her.

Getting no response he again, in a louder voice, repeated himself. Still no movement. At the risk of being accused of interference, he reached out to touch the old lady on the shoulder. It was cold in the room but the act of touching her sent a shiver through him. Cold it might well be but he knew he had touched death. The old lady had passed away, unnoticed by anyone, and he within earshot. The thought of it filled him with guilt. To think he had actually persuaded her to go to the bedroom to avoid the cold only increased his sense of shame. A shame that turned to anger, rage, followed by a feeling of helplessness at his inability to perceive or understand how critical her plight was. She had died alone in the cold of her home, without as much as a cry for help or assistance, in a world indifferent to her basic needs.